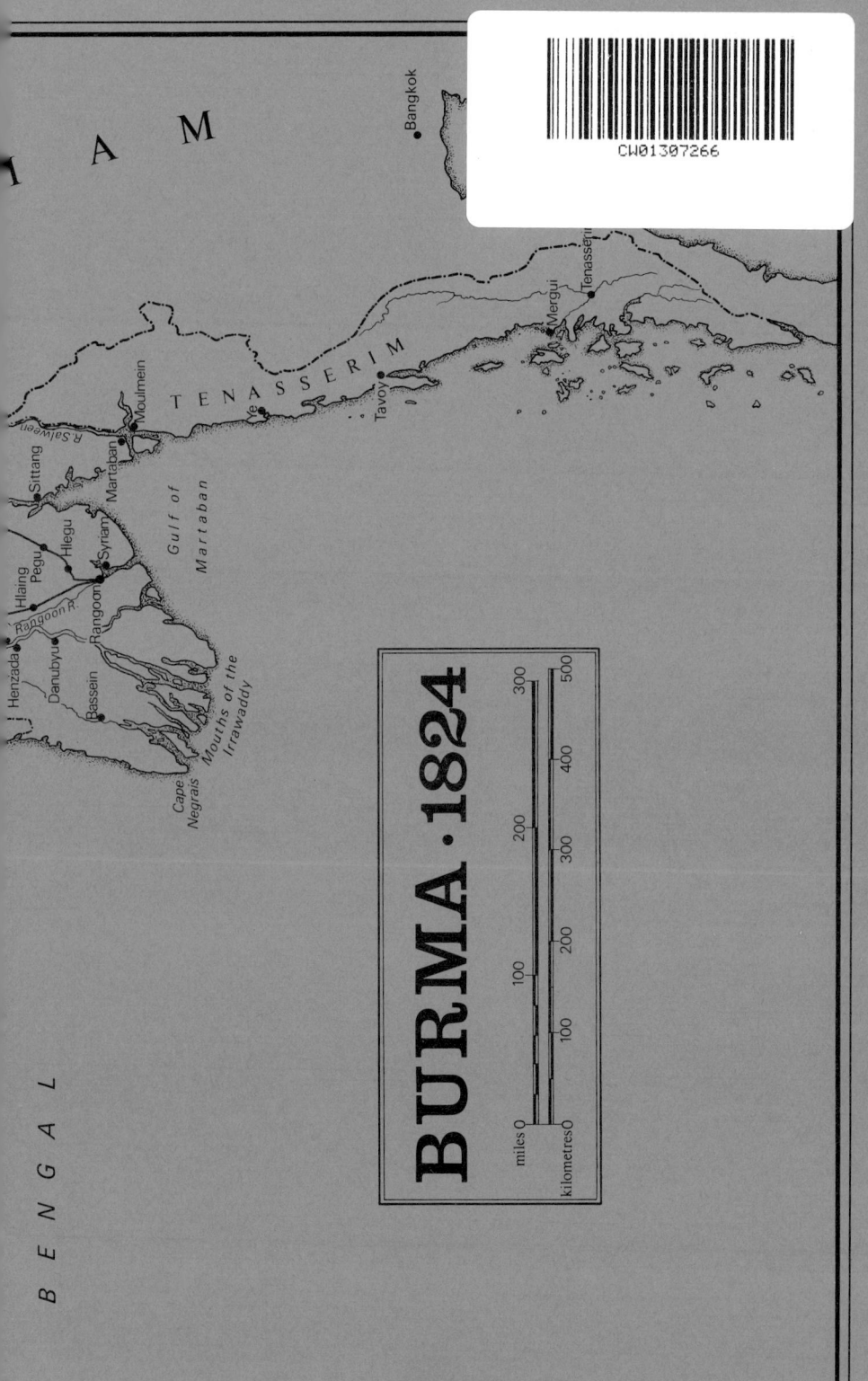

By the same author

Retreat From Kabul
Six Battles for India
The Stranglers
Dictionary of Battles
The Warsaw Uprising

The Burma Wars
1824-1886

by
GEORGE BRUCE

Hart-Davis, MacGibbon   London

Granada Publishing Limited
First published in Great Britain by Hart-Davis, MacGibbon Ltd
Frogmore St Albans Hertfordshire
and
3 Upper James Street London W1R 4BP

Copyright © 1973 by George Bruce

All rights reserved. No part of this publication
may be reproduced, stored in a retrieval system,
or transmitted, in any form or by any means,
electronic, mechanical, photocopying, recording
or otherwise, without the prior permission of
the publisher.

ISBN 0 246 10547 X
Printed in Great Britain by
Northumberland Press Limited
Gateshead

Acknowledgements

The author wishes to thank the Secretary of State for Foreign and Commonwealth Affairs for his permission to reproduce Crown-copyright material from the India Office Records. He also wishes to thank the librarians and their staffs of the India Office Records, the Ministry of Defence (Army) Library, the Indian Institute, the Bodleian Library and the London Library.

Illustration Research Service supplied the illustrations.

Contents

	List of Illustrations	ix
1	Who Wants War?	1
2	Kings of the Golden Palace	15
3	The 'Wild Foreigners' Invade	31
4	Set-back in Arakan	39
5	Disease the Worst Enemy	57
6	Mahâ Bundula in Command	77
7	Victory in the Balance	93
8	Burmese Silver	111
9	The Second War	129
10	The Third War and Annexation	151
	Notes	163
	Bibliography	169
	Index	173

List of Illustrations

Between pages 52 and 53

General Sir Archibald Campbell, C.B.
British troops landing at Rangoon
British transports attacking the Bassein River stockades
A Burmese war boat
British troops attacking a Burmese stockade near Rangoon
Combined British forces passing the Danubyu stockade
The 'Retrievers of the King's Glory'
King Bagyidaw's private ship
The capture of Martaban

Between pages 100 and 101

A Burmese war boat as used in the Second Burma War
A temporary stockade built by the British at Martaban
The storming of Rangoon
The attack on the Dunnoo stockade
A plan of the capture of Bassein
A Royal Navy steam squadron
The Burmese stockade at Rangoon
British troops storming the Shwedagon Pagoda
The east vestibule of the Shwedagon Pagoda
A gateway of the Shwedagon Pagoda
The Rangoon stockade
A British officer's living quarters

Between pages 148 and 149

The 'Signal Pagoda', Rangoon
Commander Tarleton, R.N.
Lieutenant-General Sir Henry Godwin
Commodore Lambert, R.N.
A Burmese woman
A Burmese peasant girl
A Burmese boy
An old ship gun
A Burmese war-axe

The Golden Peacock shall be stricken,
And the White Heron shall occupy its shady pool.
But a sudden storm
Will drive the White Heron away.
                ANCIENT BURMESE PROPHECY

>

1
Who Wants War?

KING BAGYIDAW's court had assembled in a state of great expectancy in the Hall of Audience in the Burmese capital of Ava one morning early in January 1824. In this open pavilion where ten rows of gilded teak columns supported a series of seven vermilion roofs, the ministers, generals and officials in long robes of white or scarlet satin, embroidered with flowers of gold, squatted with shoeless feet hidden beneath them, as tradition demanded. All gazed at the shut doors that concealed the richly carved and gilded Lion Throne.

The doors opened loudly. His Majesty entered at the foot of the steps leading up to the throne. He wore a crown of beaten gold richly studded with rubies and emeralds, shaped like a high conical cap topped by a spire like a pagoda. Huge golden wings spread out from his shoulders, a massive gold belt encircled at the waist a suit of gold chain mail.

The very weight of gold, said to be more than sixty pounds, forced him, though a fairly young man, to grip a balustrade while slowly ascending the steps to the throne. At the top he turned to face his assembled ministers and generals, who prostrated themselves until their faces touched the floor, three times in succession.

King Bagyidaw paused as if to take breath, then sat down

heavily on an embroidered cushion on the throne and gazed intently at the court. His titles, chanted by four royal heralds, rang through the pavilion like cymbals:

> The King, despotick, of great Merit, of great Power, Lord of the countries Thonaphrondah, Tomp Devah and Camboja, Sovereign of the Kingdom of Burmars, the Kingdom of Siam and Hughen and the Kingdom of Cassay, Lord of the Mines of Rubies, Gold, Silver, Copper, Iron and Amber, Lord of the White Elephant, Red Elephant and Mottled Elephant, Lord of the Vital Golden Lance, of many Golden Palaces and of all those Kingdoms, Grandours and Wealth, whose Royal Person is descended of the Nation of the Sun ...

The titles rolled on. It was a momentous occasion, the significance of which, no doubt, all those present were keenly aware. For in consultation with his council of six *wungyis* – the 'great burden bearers', who formed the kingdom's central administration – King Bagyidaw had decided that the long rivalry with the British on India's eastern frontier must be ended by war.

The edict had accordingly been pronounced and the assembly summoned so that the king could give his instructions to his great general Mahâ Bundula, though it is safe to say that the ambitious Bundula himself had prepared the plan. It ordered that while another Burmese force in the north attacked British India from Assam and Manipur, Bundula would lead his army to Arakan, march thence to Chittagong, attack and defeat the British, then march on to Calcutta and there take prisoner the Governor-General himself. To stress the importance with which the king regarded this, he provided Bundula with a pair of golden fetters, suitable for escorting this exalted personage as a prisoner back to the Court of Ava.

The audience came to an end. Bagyidaw rose slowly under the weight of his regalia. The assembly again prostrated themselves and again thrice kissed the sacred ground upon which the Golden Majesty trod. Although England was then the world's most powerful nation no one questioned his decision. Bagyidaw, as we shall see, was a despot who ruled by divine right. Like a

Who Wants War?

moving statue in gold he now descended the steps from the Lion Throne and retired from the great hall.

Later that day Bundula reviewed his 6,000 picked troops before the king and his court, with impressive ceremonial. He then ordered his commanders to stage the river crossing over the wide expanse of the Irrawaddy to Sagaing, the first stage of the journey. Henry Gouger, an English merchant, whose house was on the river bank and who up till then had not been arrested because he was a friend of the king, wrote a colourful account of the brilliant event. 'A fleet of magnificent war-boats, many of them richly gilded, were in readiness to receive the troops at midday, who embarked in perfect order,' he noted.[1]

> Each man was attired in a comfortable campaigning jacket of black cloth, thickly wadded and quilted with cotton, and was armed with a musket or spear and shield, as suited the corps to which he belonged. A profusion of flags, with gay devices, were unfurled to the breeze, martial music resounded, the Chiefs took their seats at the prows of the boats (the post of honour, as the stern is with us), and in the middle of each boat, a soldier, selected for his skill, danced a kind of hornpipe.
>
> When all was ready, the whole fleet, lining the bank for a considerable distance, dashed all at once across the river, nearly a mile wide; the loud song bursting from 6,000 lusty throats, while the stroke from thousands of oars and paddles kept time to the music. It was an exciting spectacle, one which, but for certain misgivings of its purport, I should have looked on with delight.

On the far bank Bundula mounted his elephant, and followed by his commanders on caparisoned horses, his infantry and another body of elephants bearing guns and baggage, he began the march to the Aeng pass, to cross the mountains dividing Burma from Arakan. Few of the people knew, says Gouger, that he was setting forth to attack the British, in accord with the Golden Majesty's orders. It was a well kept secret, just as were the Burmese army moves in the north, where on 18

3

January, they crossed the frontier at Manipur into British-Indian territory. Challenged near the town of Cachar, they declared that war between the two had started.[2]

The antagonism that culminated in this disaster had begun forty hot and humid years earlier. In 1784, Bagyidaw's grandfather, King Bodawpaya, had conquered the kingdom of Arakan, the coastal strip that ran along the eastern side of the Bay of Bengal. Thus, Burma acquired a common frontier with the British in Chittagong, an Indian province which the British then administered. Both Burmese and British were then expansionist powers; both too, suspected each other of coveting the other's territory. In addition, the British believed that their enemy the French were allowed to operate their warships from Burmese ports. It was a potentially explosive situation.

At first, border problems between the two powers were settled by negotiation, then in 1798 King Bodawpaya ordered 15,000 Arakanese to enlist in his army for war against Siam. Already, since their defeat, some 40,000 Arakanese had fled into British territory from the harsh rule of Bodawpaya's generals. Now another 10,000 men and their families crossed the frontier in a desperate flight from military service against Siam. Deciding that they were political refugees, the British let them stay. It was a decision that was pregnant with the seeds of conflict.

King Bodawpaya's troops pursued them across the frontier into Chittagong, where a small British-Indian force stopped the Burmese and forced them to retire. It was at that time the policy to prevent local skirmishes from escalating into war. The last thing Lord Wellesley, Governor-General, wanted then was conflict with Burma. He was fighting the Mysore War for supremacy in southern India against Tippu Sahib, the Indian leader. Wellesley therefore sent Colonel Michael Symes as envoy to the Court of Ava to establish friendlier relations with 'the least practicable delay'.

But to show that he was in earnest, Wellesley prudently ordered a suitable military force to be sent at once to Chittagong 'as a necessary measure of precaution to provide against any

Who Wants War?

sudden irruption of the Burmese forces ...' and to reinforce the representations of the British Government at the Court of Ava.[3]

Symes was also ordered to offer King Bodawpaya the aid of a British force to secure the succession to the throne of the heir apparent, by opposing the efforts to succeed of a younger son who had Siamese support. Wellesley's secret ambition, however, was to obtain a military foothold in Burma so as to make India's eastern frontier secure against either French or Burmese attacks.

'His Excellency considers it to be extremely desirable,' Symes's instructions stated, 'that the Government of Ava should consent to subsidize permanently the British force, which may be furnished on this occasion, or even a larger portion of British troops, and His Excellency accordingly desires that ... you will exert your endeavours for the attainment of that important object.'[4]

But if Symes wanted to keep these plans secret he hardly went about it in the right way. He arrived in Rangoon in May 1802 with an outsize military escort of about a hundred men, designed to impress the Burmese, whereas it merely made them suspect British intentions. He then fired off a six-pounder gun at dawn and in the evening to publicise his mission. When the Burmese objected he thought he was being subjected to a policy of harassment. He said that the Burmese requested him 'to discontinue firing the usual gun at daybreak and at eight at night, assigning a curious reason for the latter ... It being a breach of law in a Burman to fire even a musket at such untimely hours, the report of our gun created an alarm so general, as to endanger every pregnant woman in the city with miscarriage.'[5]

But such difficulties paled before the obstacles he met at the Court of Ava, which he reached a few months later. The king first showed him discourtesy by sending minor officials to greet him. Through them, he next threatened to disarm Symes's escort, at the same time intimating that a French mission which had just arrived would be given priority. Symes said that the Governor-General, who had recently defeated the French in India, would regard this as an insult and threatened to withdraw his mission. He was placated, but not for weeks could he explain his purpose in a letter to the king and later without discussion of it see him in public audience.[6]

But the Burmese disliked the style and manners of the third-rate men who made up the French mission and soon they fell out of favour. Symes, who now paid strict regard to custom in such matters as, for example, removing his shoes before entering the royal palace, was then accorded attentions and hospitality. During his earlier mission Symes's good reputation in this respect had been nearly spoilt over the affair of the goats. He had at his compound four nanny-goats, for their milk. The crown prince, the Engy Teekien, had among his collection of foreign animals nearby a flock of male goats.

Attracted by the bleat of the females the male goats rushed the fence and broke in to the courtyard of Symes's house and tried to mount the females. Symes ordered the guards to drive them away, which they tried to do by shouting at them, 'but without any effect as the animals, some of which were very large had now become furious, and after fighting with each other began to rush through our houses' – presumably in pursuit of the females.

'I then desired the Burmese to make use of sticks,' Symes reported, 'but they refused, saying that they were "praws" or lords ... and that no person dared offer injury to them. Having no alternative we armed our servants and the soldiers with large bamboos and drove them off. The Praws were severely beaten, while the Burmese lifted their eyes in surprise at our temerity.' Fortunately, the guards kept silent about the incident, for had it reached the crown prince's ears, the future of the mission would surely have been in doubt.

Despite the good impression Symes had eventually managed in his second mission to make upon the Burmese court, he failed to win a treaty allowing a British military presence in Burma; the Burmese were naturally suspicious in the extreme of such a proposal and in any case the king was little disposed to put his name to any document, on the grounds that his liberty was thereby circumscribed. So in December 1802, Symes arranged for his departure, having prepared the ground for any

Who Wants War?

policy his Government might wish to pursue. Of King Bodawpaya he wrote:

> He takes no notice ... of the propositions which were laid before him by the Envoy of the Governor-General. It seems he will treat with no power on earth as an equal, but he graciously receives under his protection China, Ceylon, Assam and the British Empire in India. He will grant a boon, but will not make a treaty; and whatever he gives, it must be in the form of a mandate, issued in favour of a suppliant ...

For this remarkable soldier-diplomat it was time for action 'I have quitted [sic] Ava with sufficient provocation to justify war,' he went on. 'At the same time ... I am decidedly of the opinion that a paramount influence in the Government and administration of Ava, obtain it how we may, is now become indispensably necessary to the interest and security of the British possessions in the East.'[7]

Symes was not so much nervous of Burmese attacks as of the French getting a military foothold in the country, and therefore being able to threaten India's south-eastern frontiers. In any case, fears of an attack on India along the north-west frontier still haunted the British Government. Only four years before Symes's mission, Napoleon had marched east as far as Egypt and Syria, with the promised aim of overthrowing British power in India – 'marching into Asia, riding an elephant, a turban on my head and in my hand the new Koran that I would have composed to suit my needs.' The Battle of the Nile, 1798, had ended those dreams, but in 1807 Napoleon and Tsar Alexander I made a strange rendezvous on a raft on the river Nieman at Tilsit and signed that dramatic reversal of alliances the Treaty of Tilsit. England was alarmed. Fears that the Corsican ogre's armies might now enter Russia and thence follow earlier invaders down the dusty roads of Persia and Afghanistan to surge across the Punjab's fertile plains into India became all too real.

India's eastern frontier therefore had to be made secure against

The Burma Wars

both the Burmese and the French. The eastern provinces of Arakan, Chittagong, Assam and Cachar were the keys to this security. Symes's successor as envoy, Captain Canning, a few years later in 1810, spelt out the details of the new British policy towards Burma at which the Colonel had hinted earlier. It was a startling reversal of Wellesley's policy of 'friendlier relations'. Referring to the repopulation of Arakan, Canning reported in 1810:

> A small force would ... probably be sufficient to effect the conquest of it. The possession of Arakan offers considerable advantages to the British Government to which it seems destined by nature to belong, being a continuation of the plain that extends from Chittagong as far as Cape Negrais, and bounded on the East by the high range of mountains that anciently formed the boundary of the Burmese Empire. The Possession of this Province would place the entire extent of Coast from Cape Cormorin to Cape Negrais under the British power, and eventually exclude French ships of war from their favourite haunts of Ramree and Chedate. The British territory would at the same time be secured from all future attacks from the Burmahs by the impenetrable barrier of the Arakan Mountains which at a moment when our European enemies are endeavouring to excite that Nation against us, may be deemed a consideration of some importance.[8]

For his part King Bodawpaya, eager to expand the empire consolidated by his illustrious father King Alompra, founder of the dynasty, hoped to acquire these provinces too. But for another few years the frontier problems were settled more or less amicably.

Then in 1811 an Arakanese named Chin Payan crossed the Naaf river from British territory with about 15,000 Arakanese refugee troops, seized land which had formerly belonged to his father and went on to occupy nearly all of Arakan. He laid siege to the capital, which surrendered on condition that the lives of the Burmese inhabitants should be spared. But the

Who Wants War?

Arakanese had an old score to settle and, despite the promise, on entering the town massacred them and exultantly marched through the streets with their victims' heads vengefully paraded on tall bamboo poles.

King Bodawpaya and his *wungyis* were convinced that Chin Payan's forces could hardly have been assembled and trained in Chittagong without British connivance. Captain Canning tried to calm them with the promise that the rebel and his followers 'would not be allowed an asylum within the British territories', but the Burmese were quick to retaliate. Two flotillas of troops in fast war canoes set sail, landed in Arakan, routed the rebels and regained control of the province. Chin Payan and many of his troops fled into the mountains. Eventually, despite British assurances to the Burmese that it would not be allowed, they made their way once more into Chittagong.

In a tortuous sentence whose implications are nevertheless clear, the Governor-General, then Lord Minto, informed London on 23 January 1812: 'Such of the natives of Arracan who had been established in the district of Chittagong as accompanied Kingberring, [*Chin Payan*] the magistrate has been directed to desire the commanding officer of the British troops to permit them to take refuge within the walls of our territories.'

All the survivors of Chin Payan's invading forces were included in this decision. Naturally, the Burmese saw it as a threat to their interests. The seeds of the Arakan problem now sprouted strongly in this over-heated political climate. A series of hostile moves by both Burmese and British followed. Burmese troops crossed the frontier into Chittagong once more, but retired when the British sent warships to Rangoon, ostensibly to embark, if necessary, Captain Canning and some British merchants. Chin Payan then invaded Arakan again in June 1812 but once more a Burmese force defeated him and again he withdrew into British territory. The Governor-General proclaimed a reward for his capture, but the Burmese doubted his good intentions. They asked Captain Canning whether, having offered the reward, Chin Payan would be surrendered to them if captured, but Canning told them he had no authority to discuss the point.

The Burma Wars

The deviousness of British policy was presumably deliberate, not accidental. By permitting hostile acts to be launched from their territory and at the same time taking a high-handed view of Burmese retaliation they were moving towards a situation in which war could easily come about.

Lord Minto, Governor-General, was in fact already thinking of war. On 4 March 1812 he wrote to the East India Company's Court of Directors in London that they had tolerated Burmese insolence and arrogance long enough and that the Court of Ava should be taught by war the greatness of British power. But the time was not ripe and the British Government opposed it. The Burmese next tried to solve the dispute by sending a mission to Calcutta to seek Chin Payan's extradition to Burma, but the British summarily refused and the mission went home empty-handed. The rebel Chin Payan now thought he saw the drift of British intentions. Trying to bring matters to a head, he proposed that they should support him in occupying Arakan, when he would be their vassal there; otherwise, he declared, he would be their enemy. But he did not live to implement his threat.

He invaded Arakan again in 1814 and this time the Burmese defeated him thoroughly. Deserted by his troops he fled into the mountains, where he died soon after. His end did not solve the problem, for the British were either unable or unwilling to stop Arakanese refugees using their territory as a base for raids into Burma and it remained a likely cause of war.

So long had the issue gone on that King Bodawpaya seemingly grew desperate and began to threaten the British. In May 1817 he ordered the Rajah of Arakan to send his son with a letter demanding the surrender of the rebel tribesmen, called Mughs, to the British authorities at Chittagong. 'The Mughs from your territory have injured and despoiled my country and have returned and received protection in your territory,' the letter accused:

The King of Ava has ordered me, in His Majesty's name, to demand these Mughs. I therefore send my son Mung-pyng-ge-keo-dong-akhoon to you ... The friendship which

Who Wants War?

subsists between the King and the British Government is like gold and silver. It is like the affection of relations to each other ... It is not proper to be at enmity, but the English Government does not try to preserve friendship. You seek for a state of affairs like fire and gunpowder.

The Mughs of Arakan are the slaves of the King of Ava. The English Government has assisted the Mughs of our four provinces and given them residence. There will be a quarrel between us and you like fire ... If this time you do not restore them according to my demand, and make no delays in doing so, the friendship subsisting between us will be broken ... Therefore I write to you to restore the Mughs then our friendship will continue. Understand this.[9]

The British were hardly pleased by this ultimatum. In a letter to the Viceroy of Pegu, the Governor-General – now Lord Hastings – blandly replied that the British Government 'cannot without a violation of the principles of justice, on which it invariably acts, deliver up a body of people who have sought its protection, some of whom have resided in its territory for 30 years.' The letter added that His Majesty could rely on the continued vigilance of British officers to prevent these disturbances to the tranquillity of his frontiers. After so much harassment it was scant comfort for King Bodawpaya.

He decided to march, but first had another threatening letter sent to the Governor-General by the Burmese Rajah of Ramree, composed especially, it would seem, to impress the British with the monarch's power. It is worth quoting at length as an example of Burmese psychological warfare at the time:

I, Nameo Sura, Rajah of Ramree, placing my head under the royal feet, resembling the golden lily, and bowing to the commands of the most illustrious governor of the universe, King of great and exalted virtue, lord of white elephants, strict observer of divine laws, who fulfills the ten precepts and performs the good works commanded by former virtuous kings, who assists and protects all living beings, whether near or remote and possesses miraculous

The Burma Wars

and invincible arms, etc., address and inform the Governor-General of Bengal that our mighty monarch is distinguished throughout the vast world by his unexampled piety and justice ...

The letter asserted that Chittagong, Moorshedabad, Ramu and Dacca did not belong to the English, but being originally subject to the Government of Arakan 'now belonged to our sovereign'. The Governor-General of the English Company should 'surrender these dominions and pay the taxes realised from them to our Government.

'If this is refused ... generals with powerful forces will be dispatched both by land and sea, and I shall myself come for the purpose of storming, capturing and destroying the whole of the English possessions, which I shall afterwards offer to my government. But I send this letter in the first place to make the demand on the Governor-General.'[11]

It was an outright threat of invasion. Lord Hastings answered that if he could suppose that the letter had been dictated by the King of Ava 'the British Government would be justified in considering war already declared, and in consequence, destroying the trade of His Majesty's empire.'[12]

For a short time the march to war was interrupted by King Bodawpaya's death, early in 1819. His grandson, Bagyidaw, without opposition seized the palace and thus was duly acknowledged as his successor. Said to be no less arrogant and capricious than Bodawpaya, but much less able, he was dominated by his second wife, a lady whose power, since she was by no means beautiful, was ascribed to witchcraft. Ambitious she certainly was, however, and she encouraged the new King Bagyidaw to follow his grandfather's policy of challenging the British.

Bagyidaw's first move was to the north. The rajah of the small independent state of Manipur, separated from India only by the even smaller state of Cachar, failed to arrive to pay homage after Bagyidaw's accession to the throne. Urged on by his queen, Bagyidaw determined to depose him and add the state to his own dominions. He sent Mahâ Bundula at the end

Who Wants War?

of the rainy season with an army that made short work of the Manipur rajah's forces and occupied the country.

Now the Burmese were well placed to attack India through the river plains of Cachar. But the British forestalled them, promptly marched troops in to Cachar and 'took the state under their protection'.

Bagyidaw in turn sent the victorious Bundula into the border state of Assam where he now defeated the Assamese rajah. Assam, whose forces the British had armed, was also declared a Burmese province. It was something of a reversal for the British.

Encouraged by these successes, the Burmese next attacked the island of Shapuri, at the mouth of the Naaf river, the boundary between Chittagong and Arakan, acknowledged as British territory through long occupation. Having killed a number of the guard on the island and hoisted their flag the Burmese withdrew.

In reply to the British protest, the Rajah of Arakan replied rudely on behalf of the king: 'If you want tranquillity be quiet, but if you rebuild a stockade on Shein-ma-bu [*Shapuri*] I will cause to be taken by force of arms the cities of Dacca and Moorshedabad, which originally belonged to the Arakan rajah ...'

The British responded to these threats of invasion by moving troop reinforcements to danger spots on the eastern frontier; at the same time they proposed negotiations to clarify the Chittagong-Arakanese frontier. A peaceful solution in their favour still seemed possible to them.

Then in January 1824, the Burmese took the last step towards war. The Burmese commander in Manipur had been warned not to occupy the key state of Cachar, which had a common frontier with the British-Indian province of Dacca. But nevertheless two Burmese columns entered Cachar and defeated the British-Indian forces who opposed them. Having tested the enemy's strength they then withdrew into Manipur.

The British were faced now with a hostile enemy on all points of the eastern frontier. It was a dangerous situation. In India itself, however, they were now secure. Lord Hastings had destroyed the challenge of the Marathas and they had nothing now to fear from the French, for Napoleon was defeated. They were thus free to make their eastern frontier secure by overcoming the Burmese. And they were now ready.

No less confident in their military prowess were the Burmese; for though they had only the smallest idea of British military skill at its best their recent victorious skirmishes with the small forces of British-Indian troops had confirmed their opinions of their own powers. And had they not three times defeated the powerful Chinese armies which less than fifty years ago had invaded them?

King Bagyidaw therefore decided that the white strangers called British must be crushed, their possessions in Bengal seized. And during the assembly of ministers and generals in the Hall of Audience in January 1824, Mahâ Bundula was given his orders to attack.

Everyone at the Court of Ava, the British learned in due course, was confident that Calcutta would soon be taken. But Bagyidaw had made a tragic mistake. He was about to expose his kingdom, held together by the fragile ties of myth and legend, to the destructive force of western materialism; and from this contagion there could be no retreat.

2

Kings of the Golden Palace

LORD AMHERST, the Governor-General who had succeeded the brilliant Lord Hastings, declared war on Burma on 5 March 1824. In a proclamation that was also a justification of this move, he asserted that the causes of war between the two countries were the Burmese acts of encroachment and aggression committed on the south-east frontier, the attack on the island of Shapuri and the invasion of Cachar. He added with typical Victorian self-righteousness that the Government had 'considered it its duty to make large allowances for the peculiar circumstances and character of the Burmese Government and people. The consciousness of the power to repel and punish aggression has strengthened the motives of forebearance.'

Haughty, but restrained came the reply of the Burmese Viceroy of Pegu, on the king's behalf. Their officers on the frontiers had full power to act, he announced ominously, and until all was settled 'communications need not be made to the golden feet'.

Having declared war the British had now to think about their plan of campaign in this unknown tropical country. General Sir Edward Paget, the Commander-in-Chief in India, who some fourteen years earlier had distinguished himself in the Peninsula campaign both with Moore and with Wellington, now showed little enthusiasm at all for the enterprise. His was the voice of reason and of military good sense. He believed that if the eastern frontier was put 'in even a tolerable state of defence' the Burmese would make no very serious attempt to pass it.

But, he declared, if he was mistaken and the Burmese armies actually invaded, he was 'inclined to hope that our military operations on the eastern frontier will be confined to their expulsion from our territories and to the re-establishment of those states along the line of our frontier which have been over-run and conquered by the Burmese.' Any military campaign against the kingdom of Ava he deprecated. 'Instead of armies, fortresses and cities, I am led to believe that we shall find nothing but jungle, pestilence and famine,' he wrote, with remarkable foresight.

Sir Edward had learned that the Burmese climate and terrain alone were foes enough for an invading army. In the hot season, February to May, the troops, clad in their stifling red serge jackets, would broil in temperatures reaching 105 degrees Fahrenheit. For another four months, in the rainy season, June to mid-October, as the monsoon's deluge crashed down like a waterfall and turned nearly the whole country into a string of steaming lakes, they would be immobilised, a prey to sickness and disease. Only for the three months of the cool season, November to the end of January, would they be able to campaign effectively.

The terrain would be no less hostile. A range of mountains, the Arakan Yomas, ran the length of the country from north to south, while the Lushai Hills, rugged jungle regions ranging up to 12,000 feet, extended east to west south of Manipur and Cachar. Great rivers, the Irrawaddy, Sittang, Chindwin and Salween, plunged through the deep green valleys which divided the mountains, forests and jungles. Altogether, for an army with its miles of supply wagons, its lumbering artillery and its thousands of marching men the tropical climate and rugged terrain combined were daunting, even for the redcoats, with their array of Indian victories.

General Paget also knew that in these conditions the Burmese army, though not so well armed as the British, could be a

Kings of the Golden Palace

dangerous foe. It is worth inspecting it in some detail. The regular army, mainly the palace guard, consisted only of about 3,000 men, but along the river banks in the villages of flimsy houses built on stilts and surrounded by vivid green paddy fields lived the peasantry whom the king conscripted in time of war. From the golden palace a mandate issued to the viceroys of the provinces ordered that a precise number of men should present themselves on a given day at a certain rendezvous. Colonel Symes called them a nation of soldiers, 'every man in the kingdom being liable to be called on for military service ...'

Conscripts were supplied with one of the ancient muskets upon which the Burmese army depended, with ten rounds of ammunition and gunpowder, or a sword, spear and entrenching tool and a daily allowance of rice, which they supplemented with fruit and herbs from the land. Sometimes their uniforms consisted of black quilted cotton campaigning jackets and a patch of red cloth which they wore on their heads; sometimes they were practically naked; nor were they entitled to pay, the king regarding them as his slaves, living to carry out his wishes.

Attack rather than defence being preferred, a Burmese army of 10,000 or 20,000 approached as near as safety permitted to a hostile force. Then, while the musket-men gave covering fire, the spearmen, working always in pairs, dug a series of foxholes more or less in line like an entrenchment, according to the tactical plan.

Two men occupied each hole, shaped to protect them against both the enemy's fire and bad weather. It held a bed of leaves or brushwood, so that one man could rest while the other kept watch. A Burmese army of several thousand could thus approach an enemy and go underground within an hour. Thereafter in the dark the spearmen would dig another series of foxholes nearer the enemy positions, which before daybreak the entire army would occupy. In this way they would gradually creep up to a strong enemy until they were near enough to overwhelm him by sheer numbers in a fierce attack.

But while their digging-in was comparable with First World War tactics and to some extent those of the Americans in Vietnam, the general tactics of the Burmese resembled those of

The Burma Wars

medieval European armies. These were divided into missile fighters using bows and arrows, and shock troops equipped with sword, spear or pike. The Burmese musket-men – the missile fighters – picked off the enemy as they could, from a relative distance, until the shock troops were near enough to attack with sword and spear. During close fighting this division was not always maintained since the musket-men, whose weapons were equipped with bayonets, also fulfilled the role of shock troops.

In defence, the Burmese relied upon a system of stockading, which though elaborate, could be surmounted, as the British, pondering their best method of fighting the war early in 1824, were to find out. Constructed from beams of solid teak up to seventeen feet long, or of bamboo for more quickly erected stockades, they were fronted by ditches about eight feet deep and fifteen feet wide planted with sharpened bamboo stakes. In some stockades a high wooden fence fronted the ditch, then perhaps another space sown with stakes. Loopholes pierced the stockade itself and behind them came platforms for light guns and sharpshooters.

In the great trees which covered the terrain over which they were accustomed to fight, Burmese generals built observation posts and artillery platforms, the small artillery piece often found in Asiatic armies called a *jingal* being most often used, a weapon easily manoeuvreable by two men, firing a ball weighing half to three-quarters of a pound. Elephants carried the Burmese heavy artillery, and generals with their aides and baggage. There was also a small force of cavalry, about a thousand, part of the king's guard. Armed with an eight-foot spear, the cavalrymen rode with short stirrups and loose rein on high hard saddles with gilded or painted circular leather flaps hanging down on the horse's flanks.

Apart from these apparently formidable land forces which the British would have to face, the Burmese king possessed a force of war-boats manned by marines, which Symes, who had not been idle during his stay, described as 'the most respectable part of the Burmese military force'. They might possibly challenge a British maritime invasion. The largest of them were

Kings of the Golden Palace

eighty to a hundred feet long and about eight feet wide, manned by fifty to sixty oarsmen whose swords and lances lay beside them ready for action, and another thirty soldiers armed with firelocks. A six, nine or twelve-pounder gun was mounted on the vessel's bows.

> Their attack [noted Symes] is extremely impetuous. They advance with great rapidity and sing a war song ... They generally try to grapple and when this is effected the action becomes very severe, as these people are endowed with great courage, strength and activity ... The vessels being low in the water, their greatest danger is of being run down by a larger boat striking on their broadside ...
> The rowers are also practised to row backwards and impel the vessel with the stern foremost. This is the mode of retreat, by means of which the artillery still bears on their opponent. The largest of the war-boats do not draw more than three feet of water ... Their sides are either gilt down to the water's edge or plain, according to the rank of the person in command. Gilded boats are only permitted to princes of the blood or to persons holding the highest stations, such as *maywoon* (viceroy) of a province, and a minister of state.

Some 500 war-boats, made from a solid trunk of teak, were ready at short notice, every town or village near the rivers supplying an agreed number of men and boats.

Discipline in these Burmese armies was sternly enforced. Veneration of the king played some part in it, but fear of punishment by death for himself, his wife, children and parents if he deserted or was guilty of cowardice in face of the enemy urged the luckless conscript to do or die. Wrote Father San Germano, an Italian priest who lived in Burma for fifty years:

> The sword is always hanging over the head of the soldier, and the slightest disposition to flight, or reluctance to advance, will infallibly bring it down upon him. But what above all tends to hold the Burmese soldiery to their duty

is the dreadful execution that is done on the wives and children of those who desert. The arms and legs of these miserable victims are bound together with no more feeling than if they were brute beasts, and in this state they are shut up in cabins made of bamboo, and filled with combustible materials, which are then set on fire by means of a train of gunpowder.[1]

While officers held the lives of ordinary soldiers and their families in their hands, the king in the same way held sway over his commanders. The least a defeated general could expect was loss of all his honours, dignities and status. More often he would lose his head.

Discipline of this kind enforced a kind of desperate courage, but there seems to have been little discipline of a tactical kind. 'It must not be imagined that battles in this country bear the slightest resemblance to those of Europe,' wrote Father San Germano.

> They can never be said to engage in a regular battle, but merely to skirmish under the protection of trees or palisades; or else they approach the hostile town or army under the cover of a mound of earth, which they throw up as they advance. It may indeed sometimes happen that the two parties will meet in the open plain, but then a strange scene of confusion ensues, and each side, without any method or order, endeavours either to surround the other or to gain its rear and thus put it to flight.

So much for the troops the British were soon to challenge. But whether or not they wanted to, the redcoats and Sepoys would be fighting a kind of total war against the Burmese and their entire way of life. So one must, however briefly, say something about this, as well as of the monarchy and social system – that which Lord Amherst had termed 'the peculiar circumstances and character of the Burmese Government and people'.

Father San Germano observed: 'I suppose that there is not

Kings of the Golden Palace

in the whole world a monarch so despotic as the Burmese Emperor.'

> He is considered by himself and others absolute lord of the lives, properties and personal services of his subjects; he exalts and depresses, confers and takes away honour and rank; and, without any process of law, can put to death not only criminals guilty of capital offences, but any individual who happens to incur his displeasure. It is here a perilous thing for a person to become distinguished for wealth and possessions; for the day may easily come when he will be charged with some supposed crime, and so put to death, in order that his property may be confiscated. Every subject is the Emperor's born slave; and when he calls anyone his slave he thinks thereby to do him honour. Hence, also, he considers himself entitled to employ his subjects in any work or service, without salary or pay, and if he makes them any recompense, it is done, not from a sense of justice, but as an act of bounty.

San Germano was referring to the two kings, Hsinbyishin and Bodawpaya, who had reigned immediately before Bagyidaw, but the Burmese monarchy was always absolute, with no check whatever upon its power. Bagyidaw was in this respect worse because he had inherited the mental instability of many of the descendants of his great-grandfather, Alompra. Furious, ungovernable rages possessed him which made all those around him fear for their lives.

His chief queen, said to have no virtues to redeem her greed and viciousness, accounted for her low birth – her brother was a fish-hawker – with the story that she had been Bagyidaw's queen in an earlier life, but having sinned in a minor degree had been punished – according to the Buddhist doctrine of Karma – by rebirth in a humble family. Bagyidaw believed this and soon fell entirely under her influence. He deposed his chief queen, who had borne his son, and made this concubine his chief queen instead. Bagyidaw seems to have been aware both of his own instability and of the bad influence the concu-

The Burma Wars

bine queen possessed over him. It caused in him a kind of paranoia which worsened still more his relationships with his officials and courtiers and was to influence his conduct of the war.

The king's dominance was underlined by Burma's rigid class system, of which the symbol was the umbrella. The king was the Lord of Umbrella Bearing Chiefs in this nation of umbrella bearing chiefs. For him the white umbrella was reserved and on state occasions his attendants held eight of them above him. They were elaborate umbrellas, about twelve feet high and six feet in diameter, with gold handles embellished with rubies, and crowned with a plume of gold.

Umbrellas signified rank. The crown prince had eight, of a lesser variety. Officers of the rank of colonel and above carried gilt, or so-called golden umbrellas. Officials were allowed anything from six to one, of painted red cloth or silk, according to rank. To carry a white umbrella of any size was high treason and no Burmese who wished to go on living would dare to. Sometimes foreigners newly arrived in the country cheerfully walked out beneath one of the large white Victorian sunshades. They were quickly apprehended by the king's police, but an expensive present to the right official normally bought their freedom.[2]

Sumptuary laws sternly regulated Burma's class system, just as they did in fourteenth-century England. The biggest gold buttons, diamonds, emeralds and rubies were reserved without question for the royal family, as were gold or silver brocaded silk waistcoats and velvet sandals. Stuff and style of dress depended both on rank and social class. Ordinary articles of everyday use were shaped and made according to the owner's status, even drinking cups, betel boxes and the spittoons into which the scarlet juice of this drug was aimed. The king's spittoons were made of gold decorated with precious stones; a merchant's of ivory; a boatman's of the plainest wood.

One does not have to look far to find the source of this unquestioning veneration of royalty, this blind obedience which sanctioned even the continual wars which decimated Burmese manhood. It lay in a fairy story which was still alive in the

Kings of the Golden Palace

nineteenth century, which was believed to be true and which dominated the king's beliefs and actions.

According to Hindu concepts which the Burmese borrowed centuries ago, the royal palace symbolised the universe's very centre, believed to be at nearby Meinmo. The royal palace was therefore the home of the gods, around which, it was believed, the sun, moon and stars dutifully revolved.

Divine status was thereby conferred upon the king solely by virtue of his occupation and possession of the palace. Possession was all important, for if the palace was seized and occupied by a rival prince or a foreign power, such as the British, the ruler was forthwith dethroned.

It was to the occupant of the royal palace that the people gave their homage and loyalty. The king chose his guard from among soldiers carefully selected for their readiness to die to protect him in his palace from would-be usurpers. The conscript army too was charged with this role of maintaining the king's divine authority by defending him from his enemies. The nation's acceptance of the king's divine right implied acceptance of his despotism and his harsh laws.

But the people also gave their loyalty to the king in his role of Buddhism's chief patron and defender, for this was held by the deeply religious Burmese people to be royalty's main role. The king's outward show of his dedication lay in the building of magnificent gilded pagodas, the support of Buddhist monasteries and his personal appearance in religious ceremonies. The injustice and abuse of power which the king's despotic rule brought were identified in the popular mind with the government – the viceroys and the officials who ruled the provinces – rather than with the king.

The word 'golden', so often used by people and officials when referring to the king, was a symbol of the veneration in which he was held. It was spoken only when referring to the king or the royal palace. Reports on events in the kingdom were said to reach the 'golden eyes'. If it was good news it perfumed the 'golden nose' or delighted the 'golden feet'.

How civilised was Burma, with which the British were going to war? Anxiously debating how best to subdue this arrogant monarch, they thought of the Burmese as heathen barbarians beyond the pale of Christendom, in the self-righteous way of Victorian England. In fact, just as in England then, an often brutal administration of the law marched hand-in-hand with a good measure of civilisation. Drama and the arts flourished in Burma. Music was very popular, played on flutes, pipes, cymbals and a complex percussion system. 'In the recitation of poetry the language is exceedingly melodious,' Symes noted. 'Even the prose of common conversation appears to be measured and the concluding word of each sentence is lengthened by a musical cadence that marks the period ...'

Among both men and women there was a high rate of literacy, a monastery school catering for every village throughout the land, so that primary education was ahead of that prevailing in Britain. Universities were unknown, but the leading monastery schools offered advanced courses in religious studies and the Burmese classics, as well as secular subjects like court protocol, building construction, and engineering of a primitive kind. Western science was, of course, unknown.[3]

Automatically, at the age of sixteen, a boy became a novitiate monk in the monastery of which his school was a part; he wore the yellow robe and his head was shaved. But only a small minority remained within the Buddhist monastic order. Most young men left it and got married before they were twenty.

One of the effects of the Buddhist religion can be seen in the remarkable amount of freedom enjoyed by Burmese women, especially in an Oriental nation. They kept their own property and their own surnames when married, they were allowed to mix socially, to take part in business and commerce, although by way of contradiction their evidence in a law court was worth less than a man's and had to be given outside the court.

As a matter of routine a Burmese woman did her best to make herself sexually attractive, wearing a tightly fitting long skirt open in front so that she showed much of her right leg and thigh, sprinkling her bosom with sandalwood powder and when in full dress staining the palms of her hands and her fingernails scarlet.

Burmese life in peacetime was gay, leisurely and uninhibited, an outcome of the people's high spirits which even Buddhism's pessimistic outlook failed to chill. There were pagoda feasts at frequent intervals, cock and buffalo fights, regattas on the rivers, with boat races between rival towns. Colonel Symes, despite being humiliated by Burmese officials, as of course were all foreign envoys, thought well of them. 'They ... have an undeniable claim to the character of a civilised and well instructed people,' he noted.

> Their laws are wise and pregnant with sound morality. Their police is better regulated than in most European countries; their natural disposition is ... hospitable to strangers; their manners are rather more expressive of manly candour, than courteous dissimulation; the gradations of rank and the respect due to station are maintained with a scrupulousness which never relaxes. A knowledge of letters is so widely diffused that there are no mechanics, few of the peasants or even of the common watermen ... who cannot read and write ... Unless the rage of civil discord be again excited, or some foreign power impose an alien yoke, the Burmans bid fair to be a prosperous ... and enlightened people.[4]

Symes clearly hoped that the Burmese would remain peacefully outside the range of John Company's expansion in the east, but unfortunately, two decades later the British came to regard the coastal strips of Arakan and Tenasserim as vital to the maritime defence of India. And King Bagyidaw, eager to extend his dominions along his north-eastern frontier, had given the Governor-General the excuse he needed. Shut up in his feudal state, from which all news of what went on in the world was excluded, Bagyidaw knew little of the military power he was challenging. But he resented the presence of the British, and believed that the courage of his troops alone would be enough to bring victory. In a private talk about them with Mr Judson, an American missionary, he declared:

> What business have they to come in ships from so great

The Burma Wars

a distance to dethrone kings and take possession of countries they have no right to? They continue to conquer and govern the black strangers with caste [the Hindus], who have puny frames and no courage. They have never yet fought with so strong and brave people as the Burmese, skilled in the use of sword and spear. If they once fight with us and we have an opportunity of manifesting our bravery, it will be an example to the black nations who are now slaves of the English, and encourage them to throw off the yoke.[5]

King Bagyidaw's view of the contest in terms of sword and spear underlines the sharp contrast between Burmese and British. A feudal state, an Oriental fairyland almost, whose king ruled by divine right, faced a nation rich in scientific knowledge, money and military organisation, in this respect the world's strongest nation.

Bagyidaw unfortunately had no inkling of the grave issues at stake – that he risked not merely military defeat, but the ultimate destruction of the Burmese social fabric, the economy and the traditional basis of the monarchy. There was nobody to tell him; and even had there been such a warning he could never have heeded it.

So Bagyidaw's kingdom faced real danger.

Fortunately for him, the British, as we have seen, were totally ignorant of the problems of warfare in a tropical country of swamp and jungle like Burma. This ignorance would cause great losses in men and handicap them on all sides.

The campaign would richly deserve its title of the worst managed of all the nineteenth-century colonial wars. So there was still hope for Bagyidaw.

General Paget, the British C-in-C in India, finally decided that to attempt a campaign on land would be to invite defeat, having regard to climate and terrain. He advised the Governor-General that 'the only effectual mode of punishing the insolence of this power is by maritime means; and the question then arises, how troops are to be created for the purpose of attacking the vulnerable parts of the coast.'[6]

What exactly General Paget meant by his last phrase about troops is not altogether clear, since both the troops and the ships already existed. However, he advised the Governor-General that his objectives should be first, the expulsion of the Burmese from the territory they had recently annexed in Assam. Secondly, to despatch an expedition by sea to subdue the maritime provinces of Ava, and, if possible, penetrate to the capital by the line of the Irrawaddy river. Thirdly, to maintain a defensive attitude for the present on the Sylhet and Chittagong frontiers, merely strengthening the forces there so as to prevent any further incursions from the Burmese forces in Manipur and Arakan.[7]

Nothing in the C-in-C's guidance encouraged the GOC of the Burmese Expeditionary Force to get bogged down in a costly land campaign. But a series of errors were to lead to this.

They began when Captain Canning, the former envoy in Rangoon, persuaded Lord Amherst, the Governor-General, that they had only to occupy Rangoon to frighten the king into asking for terms; and that in any case the oppressed Burmese people would welcome the invaders as liberators. And upon this optimistic appraisal it was decided that the main expedition should penetrate up the Irrawaddy river and attack the capital itself, a journey of nearly 600 miles. And that secondly, since it was to be a maritime expedition it should arrive in Burmese waters at the start of the rainy season when the Irrawaddy would quickly be at its deepest and present no navigational problems to the men-of-war and troop transports. As hopefully planned therefore, the campaign did not envisage land operations apart from the attack on Ava, which was on the river. And on this assumption the vital land transport for the army's supplies, ammunition and baggage was never embarked.

A quite formidable naval force under the command of Commodore Grant was assembled for the task. It was made up of the sloops-of-war *Liffey*, *Larne*, *Slaney* and *Sophie*; four of the East India Company's warships; eighteen brigs, schooners and other small craft, a flotilla of 20 gun-brigs and 20 war-boats, each

The Burma Wars

carrying a heavy gun; 40 troop transports and a small steam ship, the *Diana*, the first ever used in British naval warfare. Captain Frederick Marryat, later to become the popular Victorian writer of historical novels, was in command of the *Larne*.

The total number of fighting men first embarked at Calcutta and Madras in April 1824 was 10,644, of whom 4,759 were British troops.[8] The artillery included 42 guns – howitzers, heavy and light field guns and mortars. Naval strength in guns was over 200 pieces, large and small, altogether a formidable array. Under General Sir Archibald Campbell, GOC, Colonel McCreagh commanded the Bengal Division and Colonel Macbean the Madras Division of the Burmese Expeditionary Force, as it came to be known.

Hopefully, General Campbell had actually allowed himself to be persuaded that the friendly Burmese would all too readily sell their British liberators beef cattle and fresh vegetables, so only enough salt pork and biscuit for the actual voyage across the Bay of Bengal was taken. It was a costly decision.

The two fleets met at Port Cornwalls, Andaman Islands, in the Bay of Bengal, at the end of April. General Campbell wished to sail for Rangoon on 2 May, but now the first effects of bad planning stopped him; the Madras troop transports had barely four days' supply of fresh water on board, in the tropical heat. It was another setback for the usually meticulous Campbell, for he was now obliged to postpone sailing until the navy had solved this problem for him. 'This difficulty,' he reported later, 'was very speedily removed by Captain Marryat, whose indefatigable exertions in collecting ... the scanty supply which the land springs afforded ... enabled him, on the following day, to report the fleet ready for sea.'

But just as it was getting under weigh, Commodore Grant's HMS *Liffey* and several of the absent troop transports arrived on the scene. 'Judging that some of them might also be in want of water,' Campbell noted cheerfully '... and being desirous of making the necessary arrangements with Commodore Grant, relative to our future operations, I determined upon remaining in harbour one day longer. On the following morning [5 May] we put to sea, detaching a part of my force ... against the island of Cheduba, and sending another detachment ... against Negrais, proceeding myself with the main body for the Rangoon river, which we reached on the 10th, and anchored within the bar.'[9]

Years before, in 1810, Campbell had won some distinction in the Peninsular Wars against the French, but he was under Wellington, a hard taskmaster. Now he was in command in this tropical land of rain, swamp and fever. Soon he would learn the full cost of allowing hopeful optimism to outweigh the kind of planning which leaves nothing to chance.

3
The 'Wild Foreigners' Invade

A HOT and humid Burmese morning. From the brassy sky the sun's rays bounced off the flat brown waters of Rangoon river. Led by the 50-gun *Liffey*, Commodore Grant and General Campbell aboard, the fleet of British men-of-war and troop transports, with their pyramids of white sails, and their red ensigns flying high, sailed slowly with the tide up the broad expanse of water.

Below decks in the warships, gunners stood at the ready beside loaded weapons already aimed at the shore, with its fringe of gilded pagodas and bamboo houses, awaiting the word to fire. Soldiers in thick red serge lined the bulwarks of the transports ready to repel the enemy's swift war-boats, should they dare to attack.

In the riverside rice fields, in the dense green jungle and in the bamboo huts clustered at the water's edge, Burmese villagers gazed in awe at the rebel foreigners' fleet, daring to sail up the river without acknowledging the supreme authority of the Lord of the White and all other Elephants.

But knowing the Golden Majesty's power and his much renowned victories, they had no doubts that the 'white-faced barbarians' would pay dearly for their impiety. King Bagyidaw, 'who blessed the noble city of Ava with his presence, who excelled the kings of east and west in glory and honour, and against whose power no enemy could even draw an arrow,' would command his general Mahâ Bundula to 'cover the face of the earth with a great host, who would march in several divisions to seize, crush and kill the wild foreigners.'

And crouched behind their stockades, gripping their spears and their eighteenth-century muskets the Burmese soldiers too foresaw an ignominious end to what they also were convinced was the white-faced barbarians' foolhardiness.

For their part, the British were preoccupied with getting ashore quickly, making friends with the inhabitants and buying their beef cattle and drinking water, of both of which they were now dangerously short. For it was their hope that the people would join them and rise against their tyrannical king in a bid for liberty, but nearing Rangoon now, the invaders hardly seem to have tried to make the friends they would need to succeed with such a policy.

'Of course,' wrote Ensign Doveton, nineteen, of the Madras European Fusiliers, 'the enemy had no effectual means of opposing our progress to Rangoon, before which we safely anchored at noon, the men-of-war's boats sinking, burning and destroying with most laudable zeal all that they could find combustible on either bank.'[1]

They appear, thus, to have left behind a trail of havoc, almost as if they wanted a host of enemies.

Rangoon, some twenty-eight miles from the sea, extended along the river bank for about 900 yards, a sequence of lofty brick pagodas with gilded pinnacles and bamboo houses with thatched roofs. Little could be seen of the interior of the town because it was surrounded by a stockade made of solid teak beams some twelve feet high. Behind it, no doubt, crouched the Burmese warriors.

Outside the stockade upon a small landing stage several old ship guns served by Burmese artillerymen poked their black muzzles towards the river. The *Liffey*, having furled sails and beat to quarters, dropped anchor towering above this enemy battery, about 100 yards off. The other men-of-war and the troop transports anchored in line behind her. Silence, one feels safe to imagine, broken only by the creaking of the rigging and

The 'Wild Foreigners' Invade

the shouts of the sailors then hung over the oil-brown waters during the pause of some minutes that followed.

Who would be the first to fire? 'Humanity forbade that we should be the first aggressors upon an almost defenceless town, containing as we supposed a large population of unarmed and inoffensive people,' Major Snodgrass, Military Secretary to the Commander-in-Chief, noted, from the quarter deck of the mighty *Liffey*. 'Besides, the proclamations and assurances of protection which had been sent on shore the preceding day, led us to hope that an offer of capitulation would still be made.'

Capitulate, or else, was the burden of the British offer, and this General Sir Archibald Campbell believed the Burmese should do at once in face of overwhelming superiority. 'Their presumption and folly,' he noted reprovingly, 'led them to pursue a different course ...'

Smoke and flame suddenly erupted from the Burmese battery and several heavy shots whistled high up through the *Liffey*'s rigging. Campbell called it 'a feeble, ill-supported and worse directed fire ...' It did no damage, but it gave the invaders the excuse they needed. They had entered Burmese waters in force but with suitable surrender terms which, by all the usages of war, the enemy should at once have accepted. Instead, they themselves were fired upon. It was enough; war had begun at Rangoon.

The smoke from the ancient guns had hardly cleared when the *Liffey* answered with a crashing broadside from twenty-five of her 18-pounders. The 42-pound shot toppled the Burmese guns and tore through the great teak doors in the stockade guarding the town. A moment later, the frigate *Larne*, twenty guns, commanded by Captain Frederick Marryat, which on her way up had run aground, sailed close in-shore and delivered another point-blank broadside. The other men-of-war joined in as well to hammer the stockade and shatter the houses behind it.

'It was interesting,' Doveton noted coolly, 'to watch the effect of the shot from the men-of-war, the course of which could occasionally be traced by clouds of dust and fragments of tiles and brick as the iron missiles tore the roofs off some of the larger dwellings.'

The Burma Wars

General Campbell, a burly Scot with thick red side-whiskers, now put his plan of attack into action. Detachments of the 38th, 41st and 13th regiments were rowed to the shore to cover the disembarkation of the rest. Shots whistled over their heads as fresh Burmese gunners again served the shore battery, but once more the guns were silenced by a broadside from the *Liffey*.

Resistance then came to an end. In about half an hour two entire brigades were ashore, vivid masses of red against the pale green of the ubiquitous bamboo. 'In less than twenty minutes,' noted Campbell,[2] 'I had the satisfaction of seeing the British flag flying in the town, without the troops having to discharge a single musket, and without my having occasion to regret the loss of one individual, killed or wounded, on our side.'

It seemed solid success, for Campbell had seized this port of forty thousand people without so much as a single casualty.

But where were the friendly population upon whom the British so much depended? Lord Amherst had cheerfully assumed that owing to the ruthless despotism of the King of Ava, British troops needed only to set foot in Rangoon to be greeted as liberators by the enslaved Burmans, who would without delay offer them all the food, cattle, boats and boatmen they needed, at bargain prices.

There were many experiences in the British Army's past to contradict such hopes. Perhaps the most recent was the landing of Sir Ralph Abercromby in Holland in 1799 in the belief that the Orange party would rise to aid them; but a foreign invader can generally be relied upon to bring about an end to local quarrels and form a united opposition. There was no support from the Orange party, no food and no transport; nothing except hostility.

Nevertheless, forgetting such lessons of war, Campbell had fallen victim to the spirit of optimism that had grown around this expedition into a more or less unknown country. He had counted on a welcoming population, but instead he found a town totally deserted and swept bare. 'It was soon evident that the show of resistance offered,' noted Doveton, 'was only to afford the population time to leave the town with their valuables under the Burman garrison, in spite of our proclam-

The 'Wild Foreigners' Invade

ations ... holding out hopes, if not promises (so report said) of liberation from Burman bondage in return for their co-operation.'[3]

Two fears prompted the people of Rangoon, men, women and children, to quit their homes for the hardships and privations of the surrounding jungle just when the rainy season was about to start. The first was the death that they would suffer were they to disobey the order to leave. The second was their own belief that the Golden Majesty's forces would quickly destroy the wild foreigners and that they, the townspeople, would be killed as well were they to stay.

To Major Snodgrass, General Campbell's Military Secretary, it all seemed a bit unfair. 'Deserted, as we found ourselves, by the people of the country, from whom alone we could expect supplies – unprovided with the means of moving either by land or water, and the rainy monsoon just setting in – no prospect remained to us but that of a long residence in the miserable and dirty hovels of Rangoon, trusting to the transports for provisions, with such partial supplies as our foraging parties might procure ... by distant and fatiguing marches into the interior of the country.'[4]

Campbell, whose fiery whiskers belied his serene temperament, only rarely allowed himself the luxury of complaining, but he must have cursed himself for disregarding his own custom of leaving nothing to chance and relying instead upon good luck and the supposed friendship of the invaded Burmese.

He was almost without provisions with an army of eleven thousand, British and Indian, at the start of the rainy season, in a city of deserted pagodas and bamboo cottages. He was hemmed in by jungles which would soon be almost impassable and by swamps soon to be lakes which could stop him from making any move at all. Where the Burmese army was he had not the least idea.

It was an alarming predicament, but as if to worsen it the British troops ashore, between three and four thousand men, got out of control that night and put the whole landing in danger. The word somehow went round that Rangoon was an Aladdin's cave of gold, silver and precious stones, a belief that the great Shwedagon golden pagoda, towering like St Paul's to a height of four hundred feet above the town, seemed to justify.

The troops surged out in parties through the deserted streets in search of treasure. But the Burmese had taken everything of value away with them and no gold or rubies fell into their hands. Nevertheless, during their search they came upon a cellar below the brick building of a European merchant, heavy teak doors securely padlocked. A few musket balls fired at close range blew off the padlocks and the doors were opened to reveal in the torchlight row upon row of casks and the unmistakable aroma of French brandy.

In a matter of minutes, the redcoats who made this discovery were gloriously drunk. There was more to drink than the whole army could possibly take. Comrades were called in, the news spread, brandy was tossed down by half pints, an orgy of drunkenness followed and soon hundreds of normally disciplined soldiers were lying flat drunk in the cellar or the nearby streets.

A mob of those who could still stand persuaded themselves that there must be loot still in the town. Weaving drunkenly through the narrow streets with flaming torches they set off to pillage the houses, but someone, by accident or design, set the inflammable wood afire. The fire spread, and soon half the town was ablaze in great sheets of flame that engulfed street after street.

The troops were soon in danger of being caught in the flames, but the navy came to the rescue. Commodore Grant, on board the *Liffey*, ordered ashore as many sailors as he could spare as a fire party. They stopped the blaze spreading, but only after half Rangoon had been gutted. Meanwhile, officers cleared the brandy cellar of drunken troops at pistol point and on Campbell's orders set about the melancholy task of spilling the entire contents of two or three hundred hogsheads of brandy on to the ground.

The whole expedition was now in jeopardy, for at any moment the Burmese might launch a counter-attack through the town and destroy the drunken soldiers, or drive them into the river. Upon the navy that night the salvation of the invasion depended. The Burmese failed to seize their chance and when

The 'Wild Foreigners' Invade

daylight spread over Rangoon's smoking ruins British sailors and a few Sepoys were holding the town for the regiments, who were too drunk even to hold their weapons.

With daylight and a slow return to sobriety the worst was over. Campbell quickly landed the rest of his army. All he could do now was to obtain provisions somehow, learn something of this country and people he had been sent to invade in such woeful ignorance, and try to hold out against Burmese attacks in the impending rainy season, when his army would be more or less immobilised in Rangoon. Meanwhile, Mahâ Bundula was to make his first attack far away on the north-east frontier of India, and in an area where only small forces opposed him.

4

Set-back in Arakan

General Sir Edward Paget, Commander-in-Chief India, had decided that the object of the eastern frontier operations should be to drive the Burmese from the adjacent territory of Assam – Cachar, to the south of it, having been already cleared of them. Arakan, south of the British-administered province of Chittagong, he did not propose to invade immediately. He was unaware that Bundula's army would soon be on the march there with high hopes of conquering the province and advancing into Bengal.

So the first hostilities after the British proclamation of war took place in Assam. A British-Indian force of some 2,000, commanded by Brigadier McMorine, moved off from its base of Goalpara on the Bramahputra river on 13 March 1824, made up of the 2nd Battalion of the 23rd (46th) Native Infantry, six companies of local troops, three batteries of six-pounder guns carried by elephants, and a small body of cavalry, supported on the river by a flotilla of diminutive gunboats.

It was the hot season, leading up to the outbreak of the monsoon rains in May, which inevitably would limit this initial campaign to a few weeks. Haste was vital if the Burmese were to be dislodged in the time available from this territory overlooking India. But ignorance of the terrain at once proved a major pitfall. The route east towards the Burmese positions

The Burma Wars

lay along both banks of the huge river, through thick yellow jungle and high grey elephant grass which slowed progress to a few miles a day. Frequent small rivulets and ravines which crossed the track, as well as deep black mangrove swamps, made the march for officers and troops alike one of the more heroic feats associated with the extension of the Empire in the east. Troops forced their way through the steamy swamps in temperatures exceeding 100 degrees Fahrenheit and looked forward to their provisions arriving on elephants or by boat punctually at sundown.

It was a heroic opening to the campaign, but the series of skirmishes that followed in the mosquito-ridden jungle hardly justified it. The Burmese fought the British-led troops behind stockades, retreated into the jungle when the artillery hit them and occasionally counter-attacked at night, always leading the British farther away from their base and extending their tenuous supply lines.

Early in May, Brigadier McMorine died of cholera and Colonel Richards took over command, but by then heavy black clouds heralded the rains, the swamps turned into lakes and the river Brahmaputra into a great torrent. His supplies both by land and river endangered, Richards was forced to lead his sodden troops back to a base at Gohati. Thus the Burmese had been driven only from a relatively small part of the province, into which, with their skill at jungle movement, they could stalk back swiftly when the rains cleared. This outcome was discouraging for the British, because the Burmese force in Assam had been formidable neither in numbers nor equipment.

In the south, along the Chittagong frontier, the British believed they had no reason to expect a Burmese attack. Colonel Shapland commanded a skeleton force of some 3,000 men comprising the 13th (27th) Regiment of Native Infantry, five companies of the 2nd Battalion of the 20th (40th) Native Infantry and the 1st Battalion of the 23rd (45th), all mainly Bengal Sepoys, aided by the Chittagong Provincial Battalion and local tribal troops known as the Mugh Levy.

From this, Shapland detached a dangerously small force of 500 Sepoys with two 6-pounder guns, with 400 irregular troops

Set-back in Arakan

from the Provincials and the Mughs, and ordered them south to hold the frontier with Arakan where the Naaf river crossed the boundary near Ramu. Captain Noton commanded this small force and he knew that his task, if attacked, was to hold out whatever the cost until the arrival of reinforcements.

But facing him in Arakan now was Mahâ Bundula, commanding an expanded army of some ten to twelve thousand men. A division of this army, about 8,000, led by the rajahs of Arakan, Sandaway, Ramree and Cheduba, Bundula had ordered north to attack the British in Chittagong, while he himself remained poised in Arakan ready to advance with the reserves. Early in May the advance division crossed the frontier into Assam silently by night and fortified their positions upon some hills.

News of the advance was brought to Captain Noton on 10 May 1824 while he was sheltering in his tent from a tropical rainstorm. He determined to deploy the whole of his small force to reconnoitre the enemy's strength and its position and he moved off at about 5 p.m., the 23th Native Infantry detachment leading.

Upon some hills dominating the road to Ratnapulling the enemy had stockaded themselves, and it was clear to Noton that he was, to say the least, heavily outnumbered. 'On our arriving near to the stockade (about half a mile) a heavy fire was opened upon us from the hills on the left of the road, which the enemy had taken possession of in numbers and fortified,' he wrote in a report on 11 May to Colonel Shapland.[1] 'Their larger guns were fired from the further hill and the smaller ones from the lower, thereby completely commanding the road.'

Noton at first decided to stay and fight, and pushed on to a plain beyond the stockade, where he formed up his force. Then leaving Ensign Campbell, a boy of eighteen, in command, he went back with a few men to hurry on the guns, but misfortune now followed misfortune. Seemingly owing to deliberate mismanagement by the mahouts the elephants had thrown their loads, which blocked the road. 'To extricate the gun, which was hanging to the elephant, we were obliged to cut the ropes, but from the inexperience of Lieutenant Scott (having never seen guns carried on elephants before) ... after many trials and failing in all, I was obliged to leave it and take steps for carrying away the ammunition, which the other elephant had thrown off,' Noton reported. 'After this was effected, I then proceeded quietly with a party of Sepoys and an elephant and brought in the gun ...' (Noton was evidently the kind of man who believed that he had to do something himself if he wanted it done properly). He continued:

> To give the men some rest and an opportunity of procuring water, I took up a position on the plain and there remained on the alert during the night. One of the Mugs [sic] fancied he saw some Burmahs creeping towards us, and commenced a running fire, which was with difficulty stopped, otherwise we remained quiet. The enemy were firing and shouting during the whole time. From the circumstance of the ammunition-coolies having deserted, and the guns being rendered perfectly useless ... and not placing any confidence in the Mugs [sic] for support should we again have experienced a fire from the hills ... I deemed it most prudent to return again to Ramu, there to await Captain Trueman's detachment, as well as to obtain further information as to the strength of the enemy's force. Our loss was severe, in all seven missing and eleven wounded, Ensign Bennett ... being severely wounded in the left arm ... Ensign Campbell likewise receiving a hurt in the right ankle and also some shot in his legs.

At Ramu, Noton was then joined by Captain Trueman's three companies of 40th Native Infantry, making his whole force a little over one thousand strong, of whom less than half were trained regulars, but more reinforcements were on their way, he learned from Trueman. Noton therefore determined to hold out, despite being still heavily outnumbered. He was, after all, holding one of the gateways to India.

Early in the morning of the next day, 13 May, the enemy advanced from the south in strength and encamped on the south side of the river. The following day, in the evening, they attempted a crossing, but Noton had placed his two 6-pounders

Set-back in Arakan

ready for this and accurate fire drove back the enemy, but the day after, just before first light, they succeeded in crossing to the left of Noton's detachment, then quickly advanced and seized a small reservoir surrounded by a high embankment. This reservoir, of the kind called a tank throughout India, gave them good cover.

In face of this new danger Noton quickly redeployed his men behind a bank about three foot high, completely surrounding his encampment. At 8 a.m. the Burmese advanced and began entrenching themselves 300 yards in front of his position, the right flank of which was protected by the river and by a water tank about 60 yards in front. This being surrounded by a high embankment, serving as a breastwork, Noton utilised as a post for an outlying picquet, who fired on the entrenched enemy during the whole of that day and the following night, but with little effect.

Meanwhile, Noton strengthened his position still more by posting a numerically strong detachment of the Provincials and the Mugh Levy around a third water tank to the rear, and he may well have felt that provided there were no desertions among the non-regular troops he could hold out without much difficulty.

On the morning of 16 May he discovered that the Burmese had during the night entrenched themselves on his left flank and had advanced the troops in front considerably. At the time it made little difference, for the desultory fire of the next 24 hours caused few casualties on either side, but by daybreak on the 17th the Burmese had pushed their trenches right up to within 12 paces of the outlying picquet around the water tank and to within a short distance of the rear tank held by the Mughs and the Provincials.

So dexterously did the Burmese take cover in their deep trenches that the sharp fire Noton's men kept up still had little effect; and so heavily outnumbered was he that to attempt a bayonet charge, especially with not very reliable troops, would be suicidal. Already the Provincials and some of the Mughs showed signs of alarm and insubordination, while three or four of his officers were wounded. Noton now very seriously considered retreating, but knowing that Captain Brandon, with a detachment of the 23rd Native Infantry, had left Chittagong on the 13th and should arrive that same day, the 17th, he stubbornly decided not to give way. It was a fatal error, for he should now have made a strategic withdrawal towards the reinforcements advancing from the Chittagong frontier. In staying he lost his only chance of saving some of his officers, many of his men, and himself.

A heavy and destructive fire was now poured in by the Burmese. This and the fear of a charge by overwhelming forces now so much frightened the Mughs and Provincial troops holding the water tank to the rear of the position that suddenly, at about 9 a.m., they abandoned it and fled at a fast pace out of harm's way. The Burmese at once occupied it, so that the rear of Noton's position was now undefended. As the alarm spread still more of the Mughs fled. Fear-stricken as well were the elephant drivers who drove their animals to join the rout of hundreds of running men. The wounded Lieutenant Scott had been tied for safety to the back of one of these animals.

Noton's position was now obviously untenable, being very nearly surrounded and under heavy fire, with barely 400 men, exhausted after having been continuously under arms since the 13th. Regretfully, he therefore ordered a retreat, but it was too late. 'The bugle was sounded repeatedly for the recall of the picquet,' noted one of the surviving officers in his report.[2]

> But from the heavy fire which was kept up at the time it was not heard and as there was no time to lose, the detachment commenced its retreat. The officer on picquet perceived by chance the retrograde movement of the detachment after it had proceeded a considerable distance. The picquet was then instantly withdrawn and joined the main body, which by having from necessity abandoned the two 6-pounders, proceeded in column order for about half a mile, keeping up a desultory fire on the enemy, who poured in on us on every side in immense numbers.
> On the arrival of the enemy's cavalry, who fell upon our rear and cut to pieces numbers of Sepoys, the detachment quickened its pace; and the utmost combined exertions of

Set-back in Arakan

the officers to preserve the ranks and effect the formation of a square, were unavailing, and each corps and company presently became so intermingled with each other that all order and discipline became at an end.

The exertions of the officers to restore order were nevertheless persevered in until our arrival at the river, when the detachment dispersed and each Sepoy, hastily divesting himself of his arms, accoutrements and clothes, plunged into the river and endeavoured to gain the opposite bank.

Noton was on foot, commanding the rearguard, who were fighting off by gun, sword and pistol the Burmese attempt to steamroller them. Shot and wounded, Noton fell, and was at once sabred to death by Burmese cavalry. Trueman, who took his place in command of the rearguard, was then ridden down by the cavalrymen, who dismounted and cut him also to pieces. Captain Pringle and Ensign Bennett were killed in attempting to cross the river. Also killed were Lieutenant Grigg and Assistant-Surgeon Maysmore. Some 300 men lost their lives and another 250, mainly Bengal Sepoys, were taken prisoner.

The British advanced defence in the south was thus destroyed. The war had started far from well for them.

Reactions ranging from unease to alarm and panic in Chittagong, Dacca and even Calcutta followed upon the news of this decisive defeat of a British force by the Burmese. It was thought quite likely, though not by the British, that the enemy might penetrate the Sunderban forest and advance on Calcutta itself; some Indian merchants even moved themselves and their families under the guns of Fort William.

General Paget, however, frankly recognised that the error of overlooking the possibility of an attack from Arakan had caused Chittagong to be too weakly held. Colonel Shapland was speedily reinforced. The province would now be out of danger, it was believed, should Bundula justify his reputation and exploit his victory by a swift advance.

But apart from an attempt to cut off the gunboats on the river and an advance of a few miles to Chekeria, whence his forces soon withdrew, Bundula stayed uncharacteristically passive, even though the king had ordered him to advance into Bengal. Probably news of the British maritime invasion – they had entered Rangoon on 9 May – had reached him via the swift-running messengers the Burmese used, and such an event would certainly have stayed him. Towards the end of May he wrote to King Bagyidaw[3] declaring that 'he was ashamed that the King had no more brave generals'. He would engage at any time, he boasted, to beat off 100 Sepoys with 50 Burmans. He begged to be recalled and sent below [to Rangoon]. Later, his request was granted. He vanished silently overnight with his entire army and prisoners, none of the British troops encamped less than a mile away hearing him go and knowing nothing of it until villagers told them.

On Sunday, 23 May, King Bagyidaw received the news of the fall of Rangoon in his new capital of Ava, where he had recently taken up residence after a final farewell to the old capital of Amarapura. While the British were sailing for Rangoon, Bagyidaw, expecting no danger from that region of his kingdom, had been taking triumphant possession of the capital, which would be the target of the 'white-faced barbarians'' invasion. An American lady, Mrs Anne Judson, wife of the missionary Adoniram Judson, noted the assurance and ostentation of the ceremony 'when majesty with all its attendant glory, entered the gates of the golden city, and amid the acclamation of millions, I may say, took possession of the palace.'

> The sawbwas of the provinces bordering on China, all the viceroys and high officers of the kingdom, were assembled on the occasion, dressed in their robes of state, and ornamented with the insignia of their office. The white elephant, richly adorned with gold and jewels, was one of the most beautiful objects in the procession. The King and Queen alone were unadorned, dressed in the simple garb of the country; they, hand in hand, entered the garden in which we had taken our seats, and where a banquet was prepared for their refreshment ... Soon after His Majesty had taken possession of the palace an order was issued that no

Set-back in Arakan

foreigner should be allowed to enter, excepting Lanciego [a Spanish merchant].[4]

The cause of the exclusion of Europeans, towards whom Bagyidaw had hitherto shown great friendship, as well as generosity, was the fall of Rangoon, which whipped up feelings of bravado and revenge. The Kee Wungyi, prime minister, was immediately sent south with an army of 12,000 and orders to arouse the entire southern region against the invaders. Henry Gouger, British merchant, recalled that he was told that the king was pleased about the British landing – they had fallen into a snare and would be a sure prey. Their arms, the king observed, would be useful in his projected conquest of Siam.[5] Said Gouger:

> The whole city was convulsed with rage ... at the loss of their great seaport. But there was a feeling of satisfaction and exultation that the white foreigners had fallen into a trap from which they could not escape, and would inevitably be destroyed like vermin. Such a hold had this delusion taken, that the only fear now expressed was that their enemies would plunder the town and escape before the Royal army had time to arrive and give them battle.
>
> Their expressions of confidence were as unbounded as their indignation; indeed, this buoyancy of feeling gave the town the resemblance of a joyous festival, intermingled with fits of frantic rage. Many songs were extemporised, teeming with ridicule and defiance. The burden of one of them was singularly refined and elegant. It contemplated nothing less than hunting the British General for the sake of his hide; he was to be caught, flayed and his skin tanned into leather to make shoes for the Heir Apparent!

Anne Judson also noted the wave of braggadocio. 'No doubt was entertained of the defeat of the English,' she remarked.

The only fear of the king was that the foreigners, hearing of the advance of the Burman troops, would be so alarmed as to flee on board their ships and depart, before there would be time to secure them as slaves. 'Bring for me,' said a wild young buck of the palace, 'six *kala-pycos* (white strangers) to row my boat.' 'And to me,' said a lady of a Woongyee [minister], 'send four white strangers to manage the affairs of my house, as I understand they are trusty servants.' The war-boats in high glee, passed our house, the soldiers singing and dancing and exhibiting gestures of the most joyous kind. 'Poor fellows,' said we, 'you will probably never dance again!'

King Bagyidaw was thus by no means dismayed when he heard that the British had landed in Rangoon. Adoniram Judson, who met him almost every day, portrays him as the sort of man high-ranking British officials would probably have liked had they taken the trouble to meet him, instead of deputing underlings. Though he was dignified, with graceful manners, in public, Judson saw him as affable and playful almost to boyishness in private and curiously anxious to see everyone around him happy.

He spent his time, apart from court affairs, riding on horseback or upon an elephant; listening to music, or attending dancing or theatrical shows, but always in the company of his chief queen, 'to whom he is devoted even to infatuation'. Although he was officially the patron of the Buddhist religion in Burma, Judson was inclined to think he was indifferent to all religions. Once only did he see him perform 'an act of devotion'.

A beautiful image of Buddha stood in a recess in the audience chamber, before which, after a levée, many of the courtiers performed their devotions, but Judson saw the king do so only once. One day, while the American was in the audience chamber alone, Bagyidaw came walking in 'in his usual brisk and lively manner. He looked about him, and, appearing to have nothing else to do, knelt before the image, made a hasty prayer and obeisance to it, and jumped up again, proceeding straight to the stables to see his favourite horses fed.'[6]

But this hedonistic king, good-natured and unwilling to disoblige those near to him, urged on by ambitious generals into a war with the British, whose invasion he regarded as a maraud-

Set-back in Arakan

ing excursion of mere rebels, was about to receive a stunning shock about the true nature of the implacable western world.

General Campbell spent the days following the invasion of Rangoon deploying his men at strategic points in the town, in the great pagoda of Shwedagon, about two and a half miles north of the town and in the numerous pagodas and religious buildings along the roads which, leading from each of the two northern gates, converged in an open space before the great pagoda. Its terrace was occupied by troops of HM's 89th Regiment and the Madras Artillery, housed in smaller gilded shrines carved out of teak – homes of the attendant priests – and was the key to the whole position.

Fortunately, these temple rooms formed dry and airy billets, for it soon became clear that the C-in-C and his advisers had miscalculated and that there was no chance at all of sailing on up the Irrawaddy towards Ava, as they had planned, and for these reasons: first, because it was clear there would be no provisions to be had from the Burmese, upon whom General Campbell had depended, so that he had to rely entirely upon those sent across the Bay of Bengal from Madras and Calcutta. Second, naval reconnaissance had shown already that the banks of the Irrawaddy were defended by guns behind stockades where the channel ran close inshore. Therefore the flotilla would risk attack by night and day from these shore-based batteries. Even if it succeeded in penetrating far up the river, supply vessels from India could not follow unless powerfully escorted. Until the end of the monsoon season Campbell was therefore stuck ashore, surrounded by swamps becoming lakes and jungle turning into swamp, and unable to move more than a few miles.

Meanwhile, seamen from the various naval vessels and troops from the British regiments at Rangoon rowed up river through the clouds of mosquitoes to seek out and destroy enemy fireboats and war canoes. A yellow bamboo stockade was observed beside the bank, defending the village of Kemmendine, some six miles up on the right, and on 16 May Captain Richard Birch embarked with the grenadier company of HM's 38th Regiment on board boats of HMS *Liffey*, commanded by Lieutenant James Wilkinson, RN, to expel the Burmese troops defending it.

Heavy monsoon rains soaked the sailors and soldiers, rowing in the hot and humid atmosphere up river against the current towards their objective, but the prospect of action after the long stay aboard excited them and the stroke of the oars never flagged. Captain Birch saw a stockade on the right bank manned by the enemy about a mile from their objective. He immediately landed his men and stormed it, driving off the defenders, who left ten or twelve dead.

While Lieutenant Wilkinson and his sailors then rowed up towards Kemmendine to make a frontal attack, Birch led his troops through the jungle to assail it by the rear. But swamps and dense impenetrable jungle stopped them, so they re-embarked and joined the boats. They pulled in higher up alongside a flat bank where the troops could easily land, but suddenly with a crackle of musketry bullets thudded against the boats. An immediate attack was ordered against the concealed stockade whence the fire came. 'We had many unforseen difficulties to overcome, the enemy having placed bamboos and spikes so as to make a landing both difficult and dangerous,' Birch reported.

But in this first real test of their ability to overcome the Burmese stockades the soldiers and sailors, steady and disciplined, scaled the obstacles as if on a training exercise, established themselves within and drove the enemy out at bayonet point. Of the estimated 400 defenders, 60 – well armed with muskets and a small gun – were left dead. 'I must do them the justice to say that they fought with very great spirit, many of them receiving our charge on their spears,' Birch reported. After this action, he and Wilkinson re-embarked again and attacked a third stockade on the opposite side of the river. From this too they drove the enemy out with losses. British losses were comparatively light, only Lieutenant Thomas Kerr and one soldier being killed, Lieutenant Wilkinson wounded in the thigh and eighteen soldiers and sailors wounded.

The actions were successful, but Kemmendine itself, where the Burmese troops were believed to be concentrated, still menaced the British. Around their lines at Rangoon the reinforced Burmese forces had been during the two weeks after

Set-back in Arakan

the invasion gradually closing in and entrenching. From there or from the dense jungle that grew close to the outposts they launched continuous harassing attacks, firing upon picquets, cutting off stragglers, creating constant alarm by day and night, thus wearing down the British through sleeplessness and fatigue. Towards the end of May they had stockaded themselves in the jungle within musket-shot of the outposts there.

Deliberately, Campbell allowed them to come near, so that he could attack them without the risk of a long march through the jungle. On 27 May he decided that the time was ripe for a little action and on the next day he personally led out a force of 250 British and the same number of Sepoys, with a howitzer and a 6-pounder field gun to punish the enemy and to find out their main situation and strength.

Campbell, who refused to lower his head even when the enemy fire was at its worst, led the force out along the narrow path through the dense jungle in a deluge of rain which soaked the muskets' priming so that they could not be fired. The men fixed bayonets, however, and charged the nearest stockade built across the pathway by which they advanced, with its flanks stretching into the jungle on each side. Fortunately, it was not yet finished; and the enemy merely fired off a few shots then retreated into the jungle.

The column continued along the narrow, winding jungle pathway, here and there passing half-finished stockades, hastily abandoned, showing that a British sortie was wholly unexpected. After seven miles through swamp and jungle in the wet the artillerymen were too exhausted to manhandle the two guns any further. Campbell ordered the Sepoys to mount guard over them, pressed on with the 250 British troops and after another two miles stumbling and splashing through the dense yellow thickets, they emerged into the plain of Joazoang, a stretch of green paddy fields several inches under water. About a mile ahead stood two villages, behind which hung a cloud of smoke. Burmese troops were now seen forming up near the villages, commanded by officers on horseback, for the defence of the narrow passage between the jungle on the left and a creek on the right.

The Burma Wars

Rain went on falling in torrents, but seeing action ahead the soldiers marched on in good spirits, splashing knee-deep through the green rice fields.

Barely 100 paces from the villages they were met by a burst of musket fire from two cleverly camouflaged stockades, which their rain-soaked gunpowder prevented them from answering, so Campbell quickly gave the order for one company to hold the plain in reserve and the three others to make a bayonet charge. The troops stumbled ahead as rapidly as possible through the thick muddy water and in unison attacked the first stockade, which was barely eight feet high.

Quickly, they scaled it and attacked the enemy with the bayonet. The conflict, the first of many such, was fierce and merciless. Driven from the ramparts the defenders soon became a mob, owing to their great numbers, which was restricted by two narrow exits. The volleys of musketry poured in on them made them desperate, until with spear or musket couched and their heads lowered to a butting position, they blindly charged upon the British bayonets, continuing to fight until long after hope of success or escape had gone.

Campbell ordered his men out, leaving two or three hundred enemy dead or wounded in heaps on the ground, then forming the men as if on parade he ordered a charge upon the second stockade and after a longer, sharper struggle dislodged the enemy from this too. The enemy's main force, seeing the British drawn up on the plain between the two stockades now began to charge Campbell's reserve company, which they heavily outnumbered, until they were checked by the sight of the victorious troops emerging from the second stockade to attack their own flank. They then turned about and quickly disappeared into the jungle.

Pursuit was impossible, too risky. Campbell waited an hour for them to re-appear, then having collected his killed and wounded, which were few, he formed up his men and marched them slowly back, having counted more than 400 enemy dead. His men hardly seemed a British army force on their return, so torn and muddy were their uniforms.

Dress regulations were largely ignored in Burma. 'On such

General Sir Archibald Campbell, C.B., who commanded the British troops in the First Burmese War.
The National Army Museum

Detachments of the British 38th, 41st and 13th regiments landing at Rangoon

British transports attack the stockades of the Bassein River, February 1824, while troops make ready to land.
The National Maritime Museum

A Burmese war boat. These vessels were manned by troops armed with guns, swords and spears and were extremely fast.
The National Army Museum

British troops, led by General Sir Archibald Campbell *(mounted, centre foreground)*, attack and seize 20-feet-high teak stockades held by the Burmese—May 1824.
The National Army Museum

Led by the naval steamship *Diana*, Brigadier Cotton's troops sail past the Danubyu stockade under heavy fire from Burmese forces. In the foreground troops and naval detachments prepare to repel an attack by enemy war boats.

This cartoon of the First Burmese War was triumphantly captioned 'The Defeat of the "Retrievers of the King's Glory"'. *Radio Times Hulton Picture Library*

The Burmese King Bagyidaw's private ship which the British seized in January 1852. This 'act of piracy' outraged Burmese feelings.
The Illustrated London News (June 1852)

Martaban, south of Rangoon, fell to British forces after naval bombardment, in the first action of the Second Burmese War.
The Illustrated London News (July 1852)

The Burmese mobilised large fleets of these boats during the Second Burmese War. They were sometimes 100 feet long and were manned by expert swordsmen.
The Illustrated London News (March 1852)

Set-back in Arakan

occasions as the one referred to, officers and men frequently marched barefooted, with their pantaloons tucked up to their knees,' Ensign Doveton noted.

Many officers were reduced to the necessity of carrying their own knapsacks, when by death or otherwise they had been deprived of servants who could not now be replaced. When troops are on active service in the East, great licence is permitted in the way of costume; in fact, the Regulations could not very well be enforced where there are no army tailors to supply deficiencies.

On such a barbarous and distant service as that in question, it may well be imagined we were soon a most motley group, and would have contrasted rather strangely with the Foot Guards at St James's. My own corps ran riot very much in this particular, our colonel not being over strict as to dress. Many wore trowsers made of a coarse blue calico, used for lining tents (this was *my* favourite material); others wore white, and some tartan; in fact, every one suited his own *taste*, and all the colours of the rainbow were soon seen in the ranks, *uniform* being now, as applied to dress, quite a misnomer.

There were times when Falstaff himself might have been ashamed of us. Amongst the officers there was great diversity of taste as to head-dress, some wearing the high oil-skin shako, others foraging caps of various shapes.

Two facts were clear from this first encounter of importance in the Rangoon area. First, that British troops, with their disciplined volleys and charges, their habit of exposing themselves to enemy fire, were more than a match for the relatively untrained Burmese, even when heavily outnumbered. Second, that the Burmese stockade fortifications had exits at the rear too narrow for great bodies of troops to leave quickly, so that when driven from the ramparts the Burmese became huddled together in a mass around them, an easy target for attacking troops.

It was clear too that Campbell was an opportunist general,

over-inclined to take chances, for had either of the stockades been a little higher and had he failed to take them so easily, and then been attacked in the rear by the main Burmese force, his troops could well have been annihilated and he himself taken prisoner. As it was, the risk to his men's health by a march of nearly twenty miles in the monsoon had been considerable. But the Commander-in-Chief, General Paget, and the Governor-General, the somewhat futile Lord Amherst, were more to blame in this respect, for having put Campbell in a position where owing to bad planning he had to take risks unnecessarily.

As for Campbell himself, he had no illusions now as to the determination of his enemy, or of the reinforcements, skill and luck he would need to win a campaign, which had opened so badly for him.

> Every act of the enemy evinces a most marked determination [he complained in a wordy dispatch of 1 June 1824] of carrying hostility to the very last extremity; approaching our posts day and night, under cover of impervious and uncombustible jungle, constructing stockades and redoubts on every road and pathway, even within musket-shot of our sentries; and from their hidden fastnesses, carrying on a most barbarous and harassing warfare; firing upon our sentries at all hours of the day and night, and lurking on the outskirts of the jungle for the purpose of carrying off any unlucky wretch whom chance may throw in their way.

At the same time, he never relaxed pressure upon the enemy. The day following the attack upon the two stockades, Brigadier-General Macbean with two regiments and some howitzers marched out to the same place to try to bring the Burmese force to battle, but all he found were the deserted stockades. The next day, Major Piper and the light company of the 38th dislodged the enemy from a stockade in the jungle near the Shwedagon Pagoda, while Colonel Godwin found the enemy had abandoned the fort of Siriam, on the far side of the Pegu

Set-back in Arakan

river. The navy, meantime, in lightning raids up river had captured some sixty large barges which could be used for transporting troops.

Campbell saw Kemmendine, the village two miles up river, as his next objective; while Captain Marryat, who had succeeded to the command of the naval force on the departure of Commodore Grant, who was sick, called for its capture because the enemy could use it as a depot from which to float dangerous fire rafts down river.

Reconnaissance had shown that the Burmese had built one unusually big main stockade and several other elaborate ones there, and on 2 June Campbell was informed that they had already assembled in great force ready to attack the British lines. He therefore decided to attack first the next day.

5

Disease the Worst Enemy

Campbell made his plan of attack in haste and, as he later reported, there were 'one or two mistakes'. Early on 3 June two columns of redcoats under Colonels Hodgson and Smith wound their way through the variegated greens of the jungle, with the object of attacking the great stockade at Kemmendine at noon; the third column under Major Frith placed itself across the enemy's way of retreat.

Campbell himself this time took the less strenuous river route on board the cruiser *Mercury* with three companies of the 41st Regiment, the cruiser *Thetis* and several row-boats. The force was equipped with everything needful – except scaling ladders and a planned firing programme by the navy. The scaling ladders Campbell cannot have forgotten; once again he had decided to take a risk.

At 7 a.m. the cruisers anchored abreast of the river frontage of the big stockade and began firing on it, while the troops of the 41st landed and burnt the village and the encampment. Five hours later, at noon, the two land columns, 1,600 strong, joined forces near the main stockade and opened fire with two howitzers and a rocket mortar. The mortar exploded prematurely and blew an ammunition bearer to pieces, while the howitzers did little damage to the stockade's solid teak beams.

The Burma Wars

It was an unlucky start and heralded further misfortunes. When the flank companies of the 102nd Regiment advanced through thick jungle towards the stockade they were assailed by regular volleys of musket fire from behind and a shower of bullets whistling through the foliage. At first, believing that an enemy force had infiltrated, they turned about and fired back. The truth dawned that their comrades at the rear were firing upon them; officers ordered them to lie flat on the ground while runners were sent back to stop the shooting.

They then advanced upon the stockade, teak beams fifteen feet high held by a strong enemy force. Having scaled the first fences and ditches with which it was fronted, they clambered upon each other's shoulders under a hail of enemy fire in a brave attempt to take it by storm, but they were shot down by the score. Their officers finally called a retreat to save the loss of more lives.

Shells from the flotilla on the river then began to fall among them. 'Grape and round shot rattled about,' noted Ensign Doveton, that enthusiastic young officer of the Madras Europeans.

> They swept through the underwood and cut away the huge branches of the trees overhead in a truly terrific manner ... Several men fell, and this, as we soon found, from our own guns! For it seemed the water column had come up just as we were drawing off and, from some misconception or other, the shot that was intended for the foe was now scattering our ranks ...
>
> The cries of the wounded, the shoutings of men who had lost their way, the furious gallop of horses, the bodies of the fallen scattered on all sides, the whistling of the musket and the rushing of the cannon balls, the stunning report of the artillery and the savage yell of triumph from the enemy, altogether formed a combination of sights and sounds that will not readily be forgotten ...

About 120 men and several officers were killed that morning through British and enemy action. Crestfallen, begrimed with

Disease the Worst Enemy

mud, blood and gunpowder, the force returned to Rangoon just before sunset, having accomplished only the heartening of the enemy. Apparently, Campbell himself had ordered the naval cannonade which hit the British, for a report by Captain Ryves, commanding the *Thetis*, stated that 'all orders to the cruisers and flotilla proceeded from him'.

In the light of this and the absence of the vital scaling ladders too, Campbell's report to General Paget, the Commander-in-Chief in India, makes strange reading. 'In the course of the morning, the two columns coming down from the great Dagon Pagoda met close to the stockade ... and an effort was made to enter it, which I have no doubt would have succeeded but for the occurrence of some mistakes; and as the attack was never persevered in, I do not much regret the results, as they will tend to lull our crafty foe into a security that may soon prove fatal to him ...'

But Campbell had learnt his lesson. Henceforth, Doveton noted, no troops marched against a stockade without plenty of scaling ladders, and careful co-ordination of naval gunfire, during these first combined operations in the East the army and navy had undertaken.

Very sharp were the Burmese in exploiting their defeat of the British attack on Kemmendine. On 5 June two messengers from the enemy camp requested passports for two high-ranking officers to confer with General Campbell. The request was granted and during the afternoon gilded war-boats landed the two envoys, both dressed with colour and elegance in the Burmese court style. Major Snodgrass, Campbell's Military Secretary, who was there, noted that they entered the house and sat down with all the ease and familiarity of old friends, without constraint or fear, paying compliments to Campbell and commenting on what they saw with freedom and good humour. 'Why are you come here with ships and soldiers?' demanded the elder of the two, dressed in a long scarlet robe with a red handkerchief tied round his head, and professing at the same time the friendly disposition of the Burmese government towards the British. The war's causes were once again recited by the invaders, and it was urged that a free and frank discussion with King Bagyidaw's representatives could alone avert the disaster with which their country was threatened.[1]

Delay in the conduct of the war then became the envoys' theme, requested so that they could confer with another official of higher rank some distance up river. They were told clearly that the time for this was past and that having landed an army the British intended to fight the war until the king sent envoys authorised to enact a treaty. The elder chief coolly went on chewing his betel-nut at this rejection of their proposals, while the younger man tried hard to hide his chagrin.

Their visit had clearly been planned to gain time while bigger forces were assembled; yet they agreed to take back with them a declaration of the British terms for peace and, observed Snodgrass, 'so that they might take their departure with a better grace, expressed their intention of repeating their visit in a few days for the purpose of opening a direct communication between the British general and the Burmese ministers.'[2] They were conducted politely to their boats, whose oarsmen wore conical Chinese hats and pulled off singing in chorus, 'Oh, what a happy king have we!'

To press home the point about fighting the war, as well as to put an end to Kemmendine as a depot from which fire-boats were launched at the British shipping, no time was lost in attacking it for the second time. Campbell's losses, through sickness as well as battle, had by now been made good by the arrival of part of the 89th Regiment and two more battalions of Native Infantry from Madras.

This time he planned a much heavier attack, though perhaps not in a very rational manner. 'It was my intention not to lose a man if it could be avoided,' he reported in a dispatch[3] to the C-in-C in India. 'The country, season and roads rendered the undertaking extremely arduous but not beyond the inexhaustible spirit of such soldiers as I command.'

Some 3,000 of them were destined for the assault, with plenty of scaling ladders, four 18-pounder guns, four mortars and some lighter field guns, accompanied on the river by two cruisers, six small gunboats and six row-boats. Long before dawn on 10 June, the clatter of arms and artillery and the tramp of

Disease the Worst Enemy

troops on the march warned the defenders of Kemmendine and the intervening stockades of the British approach.

Unfortunately, there were neither horses, oxen nor elephants to haul the huge 18-pounders with which Campbell hoped to batter down the enemy stockades. His British troops, stronger and heavier than the Sepoys, were given the onerous task. Two or three regiments of infantry were harnessed to the guns and the best part of the day was spent in dragging the artillery to the point of attack through mud and mire along the villainous jungle pathways.

The chief road between Rangoon and Kemmendine ran parallel to and within a short distance of the river, bordered on the right by a dense forest and on the left by open patches of green paddy fields varied by swamp overgrown with low shrubs and grey brushwood. After about two miles, at the top of a gently sloping hill, when the men hauling the guns were staggering with fatigue, they were greeted by a rattle of musket fire from a stockade almost entirely hidden, fourteen feet high and covered on both flanks by jungle. In front it was protected by abattis, fences and palisadoes driven diagonally into the ground. The Burmese garrison on the ramparts hailed the British approach with loud cheering.

It was then 9 a.m., six exhausting hours after the start. Campbell ordered up two of the 18-pounders, which with ear-splitting detonations for half an hour hurled shots against the teak and bamboo rampart to make a big enough gap. Campbell then ordered men of the Madras Europeans and the 41st Regiment to charge, while parties of the 13th and 38th attacked in the rear by escalade.

The Burmese within fought hard but could not face the disciplined volleys and bayonet work. In less than half an hour the stockade was carried, two officers and 30 men being killed or wounded, while 150 Burmese dead were counted. Many even small wounds in this climate proved mortal. Lieutenant Robertson, a broad and tall Highlander with bushy auburn whiskers, who often entertained his fellow officers with Scottish songs, received a musket ball in the thigh, breaking his thigh bone. The break was set, but he died soon of gangrene, the scourge of the field hospitals, against which amputation, which brought new perils, was the only hope.

The road to Kemmendine now being open, the force pushed forward as fast as the tiring troops could haul the heavy guns – a few hundred yards an hour at most. It was late afternoon when behind a belt of jungle appeared a shoulder of the stockade, stretching down to the river on one side and on the other towards the higher, jungle-covered ground above. Efforts were made to surround it, but this was not carried out completely, a gap of some 150 yards being left between the end of the British line and the river on the far side of the fortification. It was an omission that cost Campbell dear.

By then it was too late to attack, in any case. The unfortunate troops spent the night digging trenches and forming batteries for the guns in more or less continual rainfall, thunder and lightning while the Burmese for very good reasons cheered or shouted and from time to time fired their muskets throughout the hours of darkness. Monkeys, birds and insects added all the noises of the jungle night to the hubbub.

Directly the outlines of the stockade emerged in the first grey light, Campbell for two hours directed a heavy fire upon it from the 18-pounders and the mortars. Feeling sure of victory he then sent in the storming parties. Not a shot was fired at them during their advance or when, in the eerie silence, they burst through the small holes in it, or climbed over by scaling ladders. The fort was deserted. 'It appeared that the enemy had evacuated it long before the batteries had opened, by means of the unguarded space,' noted Doveton.

'I heard that the first man who entered the place was an Irishman, who, after looking about him from the top of the stockade, exclaimed to his disappointed comrades, "There is nobody here at all, at all!" This was, however, not strictly the case, as we certainly had the honour of capturing an old woman; but not a man was there, either dead, wounded or alive.'[4]

Thus was Kemmendine taken and the British could at last claim to have broken out of Rangoon, but it is doubtful whether the hard labour of hauling the 18-pounders and spending a night out in the saturating jungle was worthwhile from the standpoint of the men's health. Round-shot had little effect upon the bamboo, the wood fibres merely expanding on the passage of it and springing back into position afterwards. Henceforward round-shot were seldom used to bombard bamboo stockades; scaling, and the bayonet were more certain, after shellfire.

Kemmendine could probably have been easily carried by assault on the same evening if the attack had been ordered when the troops were full of confidence and flushed with the conquest of the morning, for in this instance there was no lack of scaling ladders; whereas 185 shells, besides numerous round-shot, were fired at an empty stockade, leaving the troops with the feeling of having been tricked or outwitted by a clever foe. A garrison of four companies of the 102nd Regiment and a battalion of Sepoys was left to hold Kemmendine.

Several days of quiet now followed its capture, for the Burmese, strongly impressed by British military and naval power and shocked by their own losses, stayed at a respectful distance from the invader's lines, the troops for the first time having undisturbed nightly rest. This was of some value because exhaustion, combined with a diet of mouldy biscuit and salt pork, had already greatly lowered resistance to sickness. Dysentery, cholera and malaria had claimed more victims than enemy action, so that until the start of drier weather worse was likely to follow. Malaria would continue to be a killer, for it was of course not then known that the 'fever' was caused by the anopheles mosquito, so no defences were mounted against it. Mosquito bites were looked on as a mere irritation, while breathing the vapour rising off swampy ground was believed to be fatal.

Nobody therefore escaped malaria. During the month of June both General Campbell and Captain Marryat went down with it and on 14 June Marryat wrote to Commodore Grant, whom sickness had earlier forced to leave Burma, that he had not a commissioned or warrant officer capable of doing duty; that seven of the *Larne*'s crew had already died from cholera or dysentery, and that twenty-six more were in hospital dangerously ill, besides many others slightly attacked or remaining convalescent. 'I am afraid,' he added, 'that we shall lose many men before we leave this place. The heavy and incessant rains, the unwholesomeness of the water and the impossibility of procuring fresh provisions to restore the strength of the convalescent, forcibly point it out as the grave of a large part of the expedition.'[5]

HMS *Sophie* was therefore ordered to Calcutta and directed to return as soon as possible with provisions for both sloops and with as many additional seamen as she could procure, either by entering or impressment. It was a portent of the appalling losses through disease that were to hit officers and men ashore and afloat.

While the British were now lamenting the day that they ever set foot in Burma, their enemies were slowly recovering from the shock of unaccustomed defeat. The night attacks on sentries and picquets that had ceased after Kemmendine began again and on 25 June they floated down a huge fire-raft about a hundred yards long, consisting of 30 or 40 canoes tied together and piled high with barrels of crude oil and wood. Only by rowing out to meet it before it reached the flotilla and risking being burnt by forcing it away from the anchorage did the sailors save their ships. Captain Marryat ordered beams of timber to be chained together and anchored across the river as a safeguard against fire-rafts.

Sooner or later, the Burmese were bound to launch the attack against the invaders which their king had ordered. On 21 July unusual bustle and commotion in the jungle fronting the British positions between Rangoon and the Shwedagon Pagoda foretold the expected clash. British observers computed that eight thousand men had crossed to the Rangoon side of the river above Kemmendine in one day. The Burmese made no attempt at concealment. Clouds of smoke marked their encampments in the jungle and at about mid-day on 1 July they emerged in large bodies to the right and front of the great pagoda, moving towards Rangoon.

Half a mile from the town they attacked, but with so little resolution that it was beaten off easily by three companies of Sepoys and two guns firing grape shot and shrapnel, without the loss of a single man. This defeat still more taught the Bur-

Disease the Worst Enemy

mese to avoid regular actions in the field against the British. They for the time being changed to a policy of stockading their troops in the most inaccessible parts of the jungle, from where they could carry out hit-and-run attacks under cover of night and in this way eventually destroy the 'rebel foreigners'.

Harassing night attacks and evidence that the Burmese force was growing numerically stronger, while sickness weakened and decreased his own forces, made Campbell restless to achieve some victory that would help to raise falling morale and make his situation less galling and unpleasant. He decided to attack a strongly fortified Burmese stockade at Pagoda Point, where the Rangoon river met the Hlaing river. It was placed on a spit of land between the two rivers and protected by two stockades, one on each bank of the Rangoon river about half a mile downstream.

He formed two columns of attack, he himself with 800 men sailing early on 8 July with the naval flotilla, while Brigadier-General Macbean with 1,200 men marched upon Kamaroot, one and a half miles above Pagoda Point, to cut off the enemy retreat. Campbell observed that for the enemy the post was an important one, for the protective stockades along the river bank on the approaches to it were carefully built to give mutual support, and hard to storm without heavy losses. He therefore requested Captain Marryat to detail gunboats to shell the defences. Four of them were given the task and under the command of Lieutenant Fraser they pounded the stockades one after the other for an hour.

The enemy's guns were soon silenced and a flag signal 'breach practicable' fluttered from the mainmast-head of Fraser's ship. Assault troops of HM's 41st and the 17th Madras Native Infantry, under Colonel Godwin and Major Wahab, pulled across the river in boats, and despite the stakes and other obstacles which obstructed their landing made the assault 'in the best order and handsomest style'. The Burmese kept up a sharp but ill-directed fire, but ran off when the British entered. Many were killed, others were drowned trying to escape. The second stockade was stormed and carried in the same style, while the third was found to be abandoned.

The Burma Wars

Brigadier-General Macbean meanwhile was bogged down by his artillery in the jungle and eventually was forced to leave it behind under guard and march on to Kamaroot without it. Emerging from the jungle on to an open plain, Macbean's force was faced by a series of seven manned stockades. The two nearest were quickly taken by storm. The Burmese then fell back to a fortification made up of three strong stockades one within the other. Here a Burmese general tried to rally his disorganised troops and lead them against the British by his personal example, but he fell in the first wave of the British charge. Soon this fort too was taken.

Thus within a few hours the Burmese were dislodged from seven stockades. Eight hundred of them fell facing the steady volleys and the subsequent bayonet charges, while the British loss was less than fifty. And true to plan, a column of fugitives from the riverside stockades were intercepted, many of whom were also put to the sword. These defeats were to lower Burmese morale and will to fight decisively, for henceforward they felt themselves liable to defeat both in the field and behind the strongest stockade.

In the purely military field Campbell now seemed assured of eventual victory, for he had clearly demonstrated his supremacy, but the other enemy, disease, had grown worse and was decimating his troops, so that he saw the possibility of soon being unable to put an effective force in the field. Ensign Doveton returned to Rangoon from detachment at Kemmendine to find it 'one vast hospital with British and Indian troops alike crawling about in their hospital clothing as ghastly as ghosts' all in the grip of the 'fever', which was, of course, malaria.

Not many of them actually died from this, but it so weakened them that they more easily caught cholera or dysentery, which killed hundreds. 'Few of the poor fellows that had once entered hospital ever left it alive,' Doveton noted.

To be on the doctor's list was almost certain death. The wounded men too, died in an unusual proportion, a mere scratch, from the aforesaid cause, often ending in mortification and death. The total want moreover of fish, fresh

Disease the Worst Enemy

> meat, milk, bread or vegetables rendered the dieting of the sick a most difficult task. Funerals were now of daily occurrence; in our own regiment three, four, five, sometimes six men were carried out at a time. On one occasion I remember ten men of the regiment being buried in one day ...

No less dangerous was the navy's situation. Captain Marryat wrote again to Commodore Grant to say that HMS *Larne* by 11 July could no longer be counted an efficient ship. There had been no less than 170 cases of cholera and dysentery on board since 9 May, when it had dropped anchor in the shadow of the great pagoda. Thirteen had died of these diseases, another fifty were then suffering from them. 'Our convalescents are as ineffective as if they were in their hammocks,' Captain Marryat said in his report. 'They relapse daily and the surgeon reports that unless the vessel can be sent to cruise for a month, there is little chance of their ultimate recovery.' Marryat added that he could only muster three officers and twelve men fit for duty on board during the recent river-borne action under Lieutenant Fraser.

Uncertain and gloomy, in mid-July, was the prospect of a victorious end to the campaign in these conditions. Campbell still cherished a hope that the defeats they had suffered might encourage the Burmese to open peace talks, but it was learned later that the court astrologers continued to predict victory, so encouraging King Bagyidaw to more vigorous measures, levying and equipping men in every part of the country. Intelligence reports made this clear to Campbell, yet at that time, when the rains were at their height and the swamps had grown into lakes, while so many of his men were out of action, he could do little to press on with the war. He therefore decided to do the only thing he could do, which was to launch maritime forces against various objectives. On 4 August a naval flotilla transported 600 troops to Syriam and again drove the Burmese from the old Portuguese fort there, which they had re-occupied. Four days later another small force of 400 men stormed stockades at Dalla, on the western bank of the Rangoon river, where it had been learned that the inhabitants were somewhat hostile to the king's order for general conscription. The British suffered severe losses when exposed to enemy fire as they floundered through mud banks after they had landed, but the enemy forces failed to follow up their advantage and were driven off.

On 20 August an expedition made up of several hundred men of HM's 89th and 7th Madras Native Infantry sailed with several naval cruisers and gun brigs to seize the district of Tenasserim, to the south, both because of its long stretch of coast and for the grain and meat likely to be available there. During the three months this expedition lasted the towns of Mergui and Tavoy were captured. The people soon returned to their homes and showed themselves unworried by the change of authority from Burmese emperor to British raj.

Time hung heavily for the troops while the rains splashed down from the leaden sky day after day. Doveton and his brother officers were comfortably accommodated but passed the time in curious ways. 'The first house I inhabited in Rangoon ... consisted only of one long room ... My chums, however, being both married men, had better ideas of comfort than I had, and accordingly had partitioned off their allotments by a temporary screen, leaving me the middle space,' he wrote.

> Here I arranged my bullock trunk, cot, camp chair, table, etc., according to my limited notions of comfort; whilst sword, sash, pistols, belts and red jackets, hung suspended from the wall, ready for action. A rug served me for a mattress, and my boat-cloak for a coverlet, and, underneath the cot, the trusty fowling-piece was ever near at hand. Such was the general disposition of my goods and chattels.
>
> Our residence was raised seven or eight feet from the ground, and approached by a most awkward pair of steps. At the summit of these, and serving as a sort of ante-room to our sleeping apartment, was a spacious platform, roofed over, if I remember rightly, but very imperfectly floored, the boards having been here and there made free with as fire-wood. This was also our banqueting hall, for here we

feasted on commissariat rations, and enjoyed a cigar in the cool of the evening.

Books being a scarce commodity, and shooting in the neighbourhood of the camp being interdicted (though there was no resisting a sly shot at a dove or paddy-bird when an opportunity offered), the subs. of the army, when off duty, found the time hang very heavily on their hands. I was no exception to the generality, being quite as idle as my neighbours. My favourite resource *pour passer le temps* was in throwing a spear, at which exercise, by dint of practice upon the numerous pariah dogs with which our lines were infested, I had become very expert, in common, doubtless, with many others.

'Dog-spearing' may sound in English ears as a strange and somewhat ignoble pastime, for more cruel it certainly was not than spearing a wild hog or shooting a partridge; but, in truth, like most other sports and recreations, it was the natural result of circumstances. Spears were found in abundance at every stockade that was captured, of every variety of size and shape, so that all hands, camp-followers included, were soon well supplied with them, and hurling the javelin became quite a fashionable amusement. The dogs I have alluded to were most numerous, and soon proved a serious nuisance.

At the Court of Ava meanwhile, in the gilded treasure-laden rooms of the royal palace and beneath the crimson lacquered roofs of the Hall of Audience, the joyful confidence of king and courtiers had given way to gloom and anxiety as the carefully phrased reports from the viceroys and generals with the armies in the south failed to conceal defeat. Soon fugitives from the forces arrived in Ava with terrible stories of the strange invincibility of the 'white-faced barbarians'.

They swore that the British advanced even after their hands and legs had been shot away or cut off, and that their surgeons carefully collected these limbs and replaced them. Nor were they discouraged from advancing even by wounds and when one of them was killed another at once took his place. But apart from the ordinary soldiers' stories of the magical powers of the 'wild foreigners', which were not necessarily believed, the first circumstance of the war which earlier had deeply affected the Burmese court was the sudden and complete destruction, in its own phrase, of about a thousand men in a stockade near Rangoon by an enemy force of only about 300.

The American missionary, Adoniram Judson, who later reported these facts,[6] stated that the fugitives swore that the gate of the stockade was choked up by runaways and almost every man in it was put to death by the bayonet. 'This mode of attack was totally contrary to all that the Burmese knew of war and struck them with consternation,' Judson said.

Morale among the riverside and country peasantry fell disastrously as the news of the high losses spread throughout the country. Evasion of the conscription decrees became widespread. A sharp warning from a high official, the Kengee Awengee Bomein, to the absentee commander and men of the Yamhugangee Gold Boat fell into British hands, evidence of the enemy problem: 'In pursuance of the orders we had given, you were to collect your men, and be stationed at the mouth of the Moroon Pagoda River in the Syriam country, where there is a fort and an army,' the letter stated.

> But you, Penen, and ye principal men of the war-boat, do not consider this as the king's service; and, regardless of the dreadful punishment that awaits you, you do not attend to the orders sent, not a man having as yet arrived from your quarter. I have therefore despatched the Chief Keezee Koiznah to conduct you, together with your men, to Moroon, in order that the orders above alluded to may be carried into effect. On arriving there, let no man say he is at liberty, or in the service of such and such a chief: he that can wield a sword let him take a sword; and he that can use a spear let him take one.[7]

The king and his councillors knew, however, that the nation's confidence was far from being destroyed. They discussed ways of retrieving the situation and agreed that all would be well

Disease the Worst Enemy

when Mahâ Bundula arrived from Arakan to inspire the troops with the will to triumph over the invaders and command them effectively against this foe whom they had so disastrously under-rated.

Meantime, to inspire confidence among the people and to ensure that the generals and chiefs fulfilled their duties properly, King Bagyidaw ordered his own two brothers, the Princes of Tharrawaddy and Tonghoo, to take supreme command of the operations against Rangoon. Judson reported that it was generally believed that just before the Prince of Tharrawaddy left to take command, he had said to the king that he trusted that after driving the English out of the country, he would not be stopped, but would be allowed to chase them into Bengal, but the king, a little weary now of these promises of instant victory, only smiled and made no reply.

The prince established his headquarters at Danubyu, upon the Irrawaddy, some 60 miles from Rangoon, an army supply depot, fortified and stockaded as strongly as the Burmese could manage. He loudly proclaimed his intention of surrounding and destroying the British forces and for this purpose ordered the river in their rear to be blocked up – though it was a task of great difficulty – 'yet by labour and constant exertion, day and night, it must be done ...'[8]

Not even the vital and industrious Burmese could block the channel of the great Irrawaddy, however. In no way discouraged, Prince Tharrawaddy instead decreed rigorous conscription laws, threatening the most severe punishment to deserters and those found guilty of misconduct in face of the enemy, promising at the same time liberal rewards and honours to those who distinguished themselves in action. He brought with him a small corps of astrologers.

These oracles were much respected, especially by Burmese of rank, Major Snodgrass, General Campbell's Military Secretary, observed. They were consulted in all military operations and their decisions were rigidly followed. The influence of the moon upon the affairs of men was never doubted and from the fixing of a propitious time for attacking a position to the most mundane affair, nothing could prosper without consulting an astrologer.

The Burma Wars

Great hopes were therefore based upon the direction of command of the army by the princes, aided by the astrologers' united skill. Success could not be doubted when still another formidable reinforcement was added to it. These were the king's Invulnerables, a select corps believed by one and all to be immune from death by enemy action. Distinguished by shaven heads and the fine and colourful tattoos of elephants, tigers, leopards and other animals upon their arms and legs, they were known best to British troops by the small pieces of gold and silver or precious stones embedded beneath the skin of their arms.

Their role was to inspire the ordinary troops with courage and fearlessness and to launch desperate attacks upon the enemy. 'In all the stockades and defences of the enemy,' Snodgrass noted, 'one or two of these heroes were generally found, whose duty it was to exhibit the war-dance of defiance upon the most exposed part of their defences ...' To the Military Secretary, theirs was an absurd role. 'The infatuated wretches, under the excitement of opium, too frequently continued the ludicrous exhibition, till they afforded convincing proof of the value of their claims ...'

A strange phase of this extraordinary war now began. For three or four weeks, the British, most of them still weak from the effects of malaria and hardly capable of warding off a determined attack, were left in peace. The reason, they learned from prisoners taken earlier, was that the astrologers were restraining the Invulnerables from attacking until an expected night of the lucky moon, as they called it. This, the astrologers finally decided, was the night of 30-31 August and a unit of Invulnerables promised to drive the wild foreigners out of the Shwedagon Pagoda then so that the prince and the accompanying priests might the next day celebrate an annual festival in the sacred precincts.

The British, expecting the attack, placed a small picquet between the broad steps of the pagoda and the surrounding jungle. The moon set shortly before midnight and the jungle cries had quietened. Sharp on the stroke of twelve with a great roar a body of men – the Invulnerables – holding lanterns which glimmered in the dark rushed the British picquet, which fired volleys into the mass and retreated in good order until it reached the pagoda steps, at whose summit a strong force in line awaited them. 'At length,' Snodgrass noted,

> vivid flashes, followed by the cannon's thundering peals, broke from the silent ramparts of the British post, stilling the tumult of the advancing mass, while showers of grape and successive volleys of musketry fell with dreadful havoc among their crowded ranks, against which the imaginary shield of self-deceit ... was found of no avail, leaving the unfortunate Invulnerables scarcely a chance between destruction and inglorious flight.
>
> Nor did they hesitate long upon the alternative; a few devoted enthusiasts may have despised to fly, but as they all belonged to the same high-favoured caste, and had brought none of their less-favoured countrymen to witness their disgrace, the great body of them soon sought for safety in the jungle, where they no doubt invented a plausible account of their night's adventure ...

Other minor actions were fought during September, some, like that at Thantabain, to the credit of the British and others, like the one at Kykloo, complete failures, with heavy losses.

Meantime, the advance division of Prince Tharrawaddy's army was holding Thantabain, on the Lyne river. On 5 October Campbell sent Major Evans to attack it with 300 men of HM's 38th, 100 of the 18th Madras Infantry, a detachment of Bengal Artillery and a division of gun-boats commanded by Captain Chads, of HMS *Arachne*, whose ship had relieved the *Larne*, completely disabled by sickness. The force arrived opposite the village of Thantabain two days later, after having skirmished with enemy war-boats on the way. A flotilla of enemy war-boats, each carrying a gun, defended the village, which was fortified by three breastworks built of large beams of timber.

After beating off the attacks of the enemy war-boats the flotilla shelled the stockades. Major Evans then landed his troops and took the first of them by storm. The next morning he

The Burma Wars

attacked the main stockade, which was taken with little resistance. Built of solid teak, it was fifteen feet high, 200 yards long and 50 yards in depth, with an interior platform, loopholes for muskets, seven heavy guns and space for 2,000 men. A magnificent bungalow occupied the centre of the stockade, the residence of the wungyis in command. Shot from the naval flotilla had riddled the bungalow's walls. The force returned to headquarters without the loss of a single man and with the knowledge that Prince Tharrawaddy had learned something about British warfare.

At this time Campbell could put barely 3,000 fit men into the field. The rains continued and with it malaria, which had reached epidemic proportions, and dysentery. Convalescence did so little to restore the health of the sick that the doctors suggested establishing stations elsewhere for it. They inspected Mergui and Tavoy in the far south, reported favourably on the climate there, and these two towns were chosen for the purpose. Both were higher and dryer than Rangoon and the troops who went to convalesce there rapidly recovered their full health and vigour.

Campbell waited impatiently for the rains to end and campaigning weather to return. Three more regiments of Sepoys now joined him and helped to make good his losses. Since the main body of the Burmese troops had meantime withdrawn some sixty miles up river to Danubyu, he determined meantime to attack and seize the town of Martaban, some 100 miles to the east of Rangoon on the coast of Tenasserim, and thus complete British domination of maritime Burma.

A force of some 450 men of the 41st Regiment and the 3rd Madras Light Infantry, commanded by Lieutenant-Colonel Godwin, together with a naval flotilla in charge of Lieutenant Charles Keele, sailed on 13 October, but light and contrary winds slowed their progress, so that instead of taking the town by surprise they met an enemy well prepared for them.

Martaban lay some twenty miles from the coast up a winding creek, from which the Burmese had many chances to attack the flotilla, but finally it anchored safely nearly abreast of the town. 'At five o'clock in the morning of the 30th the men

Disease the Worst Enemy

composing the first division were in their boats – 98 of HM's 41st Regiment, 75 of the 3rd Native Light Infantry, 8 of the Bengal Artillery and 38 royal navy seamen,' Godwin reported.

> The advance sounded a little after five, and the boats rowed off, and soon came under a very heavy fire of all arms. On approaching the shore I perceived that there had been a misunderstanding with respect to the spot at which I wished to land, and that we had got on the wrong side of the nullah. As we could not carry the ladders through the mud, I ordered the boats to push off and put in at the place I had appointed.
>
> At this time a heavy fire of artillery and musketry was on us and the Lascars would not face it. Lieutenant Keele, of the *Arachne* ... pushed on ashore, and gallantly went to see if the nullah could be passed: he came back almost directly, and informed me there was a boat in the nullah, over which the men could go, and that the side of the rock to the battery appeared practicable.
>
> Trusting to the gallantry of the people with me, I determined to try it. It was stormed under a heavy fire of musketry; the enemy did not leave the fort till we were within a few paces of them, and they even threw stones at us when we were too much under the fort for their fire to reach us ...
>
> I now felt secure of the place, and after waiting till the men had recovered from the exertion, and to get them together, they marched down along the works, and cleared all before them. On marching through the town it was as usual, deserted, except by a great many women. The emptiness of the houses showed every preparation had been made ... to prevent our getting any property. I enclose a return of the guns taken, as also the ordnance stores, the quantities of the latter immense, kept in a stockade about half a mile up the hill ...

Godwin's losses were only seven killed and fourteen wounded; also two sailors were killed and three wounded. The captured ordnance stores included 16 guns, 100 jingals, 500 muskets, 7,000 round-shot, 1,500 grape-shot, 100,000 musket balls, 9,000 lbs of lead, 20,000 flints, 10,000 musket cartridges and 26,500 lbs of gunpowder. Even more worthwhile, they found large stores of grain.

Godwin had now seized all the Burmese sea coast south of Rangoon. All this, and the capture of Martaban's seemingly impregnable fort, had been achieved by an actual fighting force of 220 men. For Campbell it was good news, badly needed, for in October sickness had been the worst so far and the number of deaths the highest yet. A total of 1,200 had died from one disease or the other. And only 1,300 British troops were fit for duty. Fortunately, all the country between Rangoon and Danubyu was more or less one great lake, so that even had the Burmese been ready to exploit the enemy's weakness, of which they were no doubt aware, it would have been hard for them to do so.

For some weeks Campbell had received reports, largely through prisoners or discontented Burmese civilians who volunteered the information, that Bundula himself had arrived in Ava and was assembling an army to reinforce the Burmese forces already at Danubyu. So at last, with the return of fine weather, came the prospect of getting to grips with the enemy's main army.

6
Mahâ Bundula in Command

Mahâ Bundula had ordered his army to march across the Arakan Yomas in detached parties and assemble at Danubyu while he went on to Ava to receive King Bagyidaw's commands. During the worst of the rains, in August, the detachments of this 6,000 strong force marched down the flat coast of Arakan and then turned left and ascended the tumbled hills of the An Pass into Burma. It was a formidable task at that time of year, even for men native to the country. A thick mist hung over the hills of rain-soaked jungle, water streamed down from the leaden skies, damp air chilled the bones, mountain streams were in flood, legions of leeches sucked the blood, mosquitoes poisoned it with an especially virulent form of malaria. Many soldiers of this army, provided with only a bag of rice in the uninhabited jungle, fell by the wayside, but most of them resolutely struggled through to their rendezvous, inspired by the ferocious will of their leader.

Bundula was as unlike the ordinary Burmese general as a tiger is a sloth. Protocol, and the worship of caste, court etiquette and formal behaviour, he disdained, not perhaps on rational grounds, but because he was so individual and volcanic in character that he could not accept such restraints. He was ungovernably violent. Once, faced by a reluctant general, he was reported to have leapt from his horse and decapitated the man with a stroke of his sword. Disobedience in the ranks met equal severity. Yet he was more than a violent tyrant, for the ordinary Burmese soldiery were said to be devoted to him and much of his power arose from their willingness to fulfil his commands to the letter. Perhaps the threat of death for disobedience influenced them, but apart from his rank, he certainly exercised a strange power over men. As a result, his troops invariably took up their battle positions on time, in contrast to the leisurely methods of his fellow commanders. Alone among Burmese generals he acted according to the military situation rather than the astrologers' word. In so far as swiftness, forethought and energy marked all his campaigns, he was a man born for warfare.

Bundula was back in Ava about mid-August and was acclaimed after his victory at Ramu as a national saviour. He had with him some 250 Sepoy prisoners-of-war, still wearing their red tunics and white trousers. Before the king and his court they demonstrated items of infantry drill, like firing and reloading on the march, their obvious skill making a great impression on the assembled Burmese, who recalled that the British troops were reputed to be even better. How much greater then must their own military skill be to defeat troops like this, they reasoned. And this reassurance went far to obscure the effect of their own defeats in the Rangoon region.[1]

A much chastened Prince Tharrawaddy, whom King Bagyidaw had recalled, warned Bundula that he might find war with the British very different from his expectations. Bundula is said to have laughed, and replied· 'In eight days I will have taken my dinner in the Rungdon [public hall] of Rangoon and have returned thanks at the Shwedagon pagoda.' The prince replied: 'In a few days I shall hear of your running away, for you have a very rough people to deal with.' Nevertheless, the whole court and capital looked forward to a quick victory and a hundred guns were set up on the river bank at Ava ready to fire a victory salute.

Three months the Burmese had spent in assembling and organising the military resources of the nation; these and the troops back from Arakan had placed an army 60,000 strong,

Mahâ Bundula in Command

thought to be the biggest and best ever, at Bundula's disposal. It included 35,000 musketeers; several hundred jingals, the small highly mobile swivel guns which fired a 12-ounce ball; 700 cavalrymen from Manipur, known as the Cassay Horse, riding the short-legged but very strong horses which gave them that name; a considerable force of artillery, carried on elephant back, and some 20,000 infantry armed with swords and spears plus the necessary tools for entrenching and stockading. Finally, there was the inevitable unit of Invulnerables 'who, amply provided with charms, spells and opium ... afforded much amusement in the dance of defiance ... with the most prodigal exposure of their persons,' Snodgrass noted primly.

In the middle of November, despite rumours of Bundula's advance, Campbell too was making preparations to carry the war deeper into enemy territory, towards Ava. A group of 500 Mugh boatmen had arrived from Chittagong for river transport; two British regiments, the 1st and the 47th, some battalions of native infantry, a regiment of cavalry, a troop of horse artillery and a rocket unit were coming as reinforcements.

Then towards the end of November the British intercepted a dispatch from Bundula to the ex-governor of Martaban, which reported that he had left Prome, about 220 miles north of Rangoon on the Irrawaddy, at the head of an invincible host, with horses and elephants and all warlike stores needed to capture the English or drive them into the sea.

The British were delighted at the prospect of at last meeting the Burmese in open battle, but Campbell was by no means ready. His force was still weakened by sickness, it was still existing mainly on salt pork and mouldy biscuit, with unripe pineapples from the forests; Godwin's force had not yet returned from Martaban, and Kemmendine was only sparsely occupied. Linear defence of the extensive position between Rangoon and the Shwedagon Pagoda, two fronts each two miles long, was therefore hardly practicable.

Two lines of small posts fronting east to west, consisting of redoubts and fortified pagodas held by small garrisons with ample artillery, were therefore hurriedly built instead, leaving a reserve force ready to move to the support of any hard-pressed post. Kemmendine was supported on the river by the sloop HMS *Sophie*, 18 guns, an East India Company's cruiser and a strong flotilla of small gunboats.

By 30 November, Bundula had deployed his army in the forest before the Shwedagon Pagoda, a semi-circular ring of campfire smoke above the dark green trees marking its line, which ran from above Kemmendine in a south-easterly direction to the Pozundaung Creek below Rangoon.

With a heavy cannonade and a rattle of musketry, Bundula launched the attack on Kemmendine shortly after dawn on 1 December. 'From our commanding position on the Great Pagoda, though nearly two miles distant ... we could distinctly hear the yells and shouts of the infuriated assailants, occasionally returned by the hearty cheer of the British seamen, as they poured in their heavy broadsides upon the resolute and persevering masses,' Snodgrass reported.

At the same time, in the half light, a flotilla of fire-rafts came blazing down river from above Kemmendine, their flames, thirty or forty feet high, lighting up the jungle with a lurid glow. The East India Company's cruiser *Teignmouth*, stationed above Kemmendine for the very purpose of intercepting these rafts, upped anchor and drifted down to Rangoon out of harm's way, followed by the flaming rafts. Close behind them came a squadron of gilded war-boats, their oars flashing in unison in and out of the water. It drew up abreast of the Kemmendine stockade and opened fire on it with guns.

Major Yates, 26th Madras Native Infantry, who was in command, turned his artillery on them, but was then attacked by Burmese troops from the surrounding jungle on the land side. His musketeers held these at bay while his guns forced the war-boats to sheer off. Meanwhile, the fire-boats had run aground at a bend in the river, where happily they burnt out. This first crisis ended with the re-appearance of the *Teignmouth*, which Captain Ryves, of HMS *Sophie*, had ordered to return immediately to its station. But for Major Yates the Kemmendine situation still remained dangerous; he had only 87 British troops and some 200 Sepoys with which to hold the fort, with naval help.

Mahâ Bundula in Command

During the afternoon the sun's rays glittered on the gilt umbrellas of the commanders of five or six Burmese columns marching across the Dalla plain on the far side of the river in the direction of Rangoon. Opposite the town they began entrenching and setting up batteries with which to attack the naval vessels, while others built a stockade around the guns. Meantime for Yates, at Kemmendine, the situation was growing hotter; the Burmese had by now completely surrounded and isolated the stockade and were keeping up a persistent fire from the surrounding jungle.

Later in the afternoon, Bundula's strategy became clear. More columns of Burmese troops emerged from the forest about a mile in front of the eastern side of the Shwedagon Pagoda and with banners and flags flying took up positions along a line atop a woody ridge within gun-shot of Rangoon, extending to the river at Pozundaung Creek on the far side of it. 'In the course of a few hours we thus found ourselves completely surrounded, with the narrow channel of the Rangoon river alone unoccupied in our rear, and with only the limited space within our lines that we could still call our own,' noted Snodgrass. Bundula's left stretched from Pozundaung to the Pagoda, his centre from the Pagoda to Kemmendine and his right on the far river bank at Dalla, from which the British had withdrawn. His plan was clearly to drive the navy from the river and having thus cut the army's communications with the outer world, to overwhelm it or starve it into surrender. It was a clever plan, but all depended on the gunnery from Dalla, the fire-rafts and the war-boats.

The Burmese troops between the Pagoda and Rangoon now began to dig themselves in so energetically that in two hours they had entirely disappeared, a parapet of earth only marking their whereabouts, except for the occasional gilt umbrella of a commander as he moved about inspecting progress. 'By a distant observer,' noted Snodgrass, 'the hills, covered with mounds of earth, would have been taken for anything rather than the approaches of an attacking army; but to us who had watched the whole strange proceeding, it seemed the work of magic or enchantment.'

The Burma Wars

It was a method of warfare, amazing to the British, that nearly a hundred years later was to dominate the fighting fronts in the most destructive war the world had ever known.

But how effective were the Burmese entrenchments? During the afternoon of the 1st, Campbell decided to find out and ordered Major Sale with detachments of HM's 13th and the 18th Madras Native Infantry to make a sudden raid on the busy enemy near the Pagoda. Sale easily broke through in a surprise attack, took the enemy in flank and drove them all from their cover with considerable losses. Loaded with enemy arms, he quickly retired before they were ready to counter-attack. He brought back valuable information about the trenches and the shelter from gunfire they gave.

At Kemmendine, Major Yates and his force still held out, having driven off repeated enemy attacks. The defenders had been besieged and without rest for thirty-six hours and when darkness fell they hoped for a chance to sleep, but the Burmese favoured night attacks and around 8 p.m. in the darkness their resonant gongs sounded the assembly. Soon after, they emerged in great force from the pitch-black jungle to try to storm the stockade in the British way, by escalade. At the same time, flames of a flotilla of fire-rafts lit up the night, with which the Burmese hoped to drive off or destroy the ships and boats supporting Kemmendine by river. Partly, they succeeded; for once more the *Teignmouth* dropped down river.

The flames helped Yates in the stockade to see his enemy, so that he was able to hold his fire until the Burmese were within some 30 yards. He then opened up with grape-shot and musketry and with a little difficulty again managed to drive them off. Seamen ran the fire-rafts aground; none of them did harm. The Burmese, it was noted, advanced when attacking more or less like an uncontrolled horde and hated to expose themselves to enemy shooting. By contrast, even the humblest British soldier or Sepoy understood that advance in formation with volley firing was necessary before any attempt to storm an objective.

So that night too, Kemmendine held out, but daybreak revealed that under cover of darkness the Burmese had pushed forward their trenches amid the clumps of yellow bamboo to

Mahâ Bundula in Command

within 50 yards of the stockade, from where they were able to keep up a steady and accurate fire. Yates and his force were now hard-pressed indeed but fortunately the navy came to their rescue.

Lieutenant Kellett, of HMS *Arachne*, arrived in the river abreast of Kemmendine in his ship's pinnace, together with three row-boats loaded with seamen. Taking in the dangerous situation, he turned the pinnace guns on the enemy flanks and showered them with grape-shot at short range. The Burmese, who had then reached the stockade walls and were trying to escalade it, were shot down in large numbers and forced back to their trenches. Again Yates had survived.

The *Teignmouth* returned from Rangoon, but came under fire from the guns of the enemy war-boats, which also attacked Lieutenant Kellett's boats, while the Burmese renewed their all-out efforts to storm the stockade. In the afternoon, Yates and the defenders were once more hard-pressed, as masses of Burmese poured in their fire, both from the ground and from surrounding trees. Shelter within the stockade no longer existed and casualties began to weaken Yates's force seriously.

The bamboo and dry grass hut that sheltered Doveton and several other officers was riddled by the enemy's shot, 'and many of our native servants were so paralysed by fear, that for safety they were accustomed to jam themselves in amongst their masters' bullock trunks, and continue immovable the greater part of the day, much to our inconvenience,' he wrote.

> To be sure the missiles of our adversaries were sufficiently troublesome, and our lives were then held by a very precarious tenure. Musket-balls are no respectors either of things or persons, and proofs of this we now had every hour. In one instance, when washing my hands in the morning, a shot smashed an earthen jar containing water close to me; on another occasion, at night, a jingal-ball shattered a large glass table-shade (used in India to screen the candles from the wind) upon the mess-table of the 26th Regt, at the time (if I rightly remember) the officers were assembled at dinner.

But these are trifles, and are merely recorded here to show the inconvenient interruptions to which we were liable, even at our most social hours. It was a beautiful and interesting sight to watch the course of the shells, which we frequently discharged at night from a small bomb-vessel anchored off the place; these passed over our heads like meteors or falling stars, and exploded in the enemy's entrenchments, the effect of which, in the darkness, was very grand.

Again, after dark on 2 December resonant voices of enemy gongs and drums summoned the Burmese to attack. Carrying scaling ladders they rushed the stockade in the darkness in still another resolute attempt to force an entry and overwhelm the scanty defenders. Once more they were beaten off; they rallied and tried again and during this second effort the flames of more fire-boats again lit up the struggle and enabled Yates to turn his guns with greater effect on them. Again they were driven back, this time with heavy losses. They tried a third time, but now they were less resolute, were easily driven off and for the time being they made no more night attacks, but instead merely harassed the defenders with constant musket fire.

Shortly after dawn, the 18-gun *Sophie* anchored off Kemmendine to give what aid she could; and soon the truant *Teignmouth* returned, only to be set afire almost at once by another fire-raft, though it was put out after doing only little damage. The skirmishing Burmese war-boatsmen had by now observed that their shot went farther than the guns on the small British gun-boats. They began to hit the sailors in them and make harder Kellett's task of firing on the troops attacking Kemmendine from the flank, which the Burmese continued throughout 3 December.

Kellett therefore assembled a flotilla of eight boats with some 80 seamen and several midshipmen and in the cool dawn of 4 December made a dash at the gilded war-boats, captured seven of them and drove off the rest up river. One of the war-boats taken, mounting a long 9-pounder on the bow, was 96 feet long with places for 76 oarsmen.[2]

On the night of 4 December the Burmese attacked the Kem-

Mahâ Bundula in Command

mendine stockade once more in a final effort to master it. Several times they were thrown back, until finally they gave up, having lost heart, realising perhaps that their own stockades, when held by the 'wild foreigners', were invulnerable. And from then on Kemmendine was in no real danger. The key stockade had survived the worst the Burmese could do.

'The unyielding spirit of Major Yates and his steady troops, although exhausted with fatigue and want of rest, baffled every attempt on shore,' reported General Campbell later, in a message to the Governor-General, 'while Captain Ryves, with HM's sloop *Sophie*, the H.C. cruiser *Teignmouth* and some flotilla and gun-boats, nobly maintained the long established fame of the British navy, in defending the passage of the river against the most furious assaults of the enemy's war-boats, advancing under cover of the most tremendous fire-rafts which the unwearied exertions of British sailors could alone have conquered.'

Campbell's dispatches became famed for their ringing note of praise for his own operations, as if he had won victories outstanding in the annals of the British Empire. Probably he was right; it was no mean feat at that time to make war successfully against a bold enemy defending his own territory of disease-ridden swamp, forest and jungle, thus to add a new realm to the Empire.

Meantime, between Rangoon and the Pagoda, Campbell had let the enemy deploy in force with as much stores as they could bring up, so that when he finally attacked them their loss would be all the greater. By daylight on the morning of 2 December they had completely entrenched themselves upon some high and open ground within musket-shot distance of the Pagoda's north side. Several times British skirmishers dislodged them from positions which enabled their guns to enfilade the British line, or their musket shot to hit troops asleep in barracks.

But the Burmese burrowed like moles, with unremitting energy, by the evening of 4 December being so near the Pagoda that they were able, Snodgrass noted, to keep up 'a constant fire upon our barracks, saluting with a dozen muskets every one who showed his head above the ramparts, and, when nothing better could be done, expending both round and grape-shot in vain

The Burma Wars

attempts to strike the British ensign, which proudly waved high upon their sacred temple.'

They were near enough to Rangoon as well to fire an occasional gun at it, and from the opposite side of the river they poured an endless stream of fire against the ships. With the exception of one or two heavily armed ones, which fired back, they anchored as near as possible to Rangoon to lessen the chance of damage.

On the evening of 4 December Campbell at last revealed his plan for a decisive counter-blow. Before dawn next day Captain Chads accordingly moved up Pozundaung Creek with the gun-flotilla and cannonaded the enemy's left rear at daylight, while shortly afterwards 1,100 men under Major Sale, and 600 under Major Walker, attacked the Burmese centre and left respectively.

Walker reached his objective first and here the Burmese, despite naval shelling, fought desperately. Walker and many men fell in the advance to the first entrenchment, but it was finally carried at bayonet point and the enemy routed. Sale's column then reached the centre and quickly forced it, so that the entire Burmese left wing was scattered. The two British columns then drove the defenders from every part of their works into the jungle, leaving the ground behind them covered with dead and wounded, with all their guns, entrenching tools, and a great number of small arms. So quickly were the attacks delivered that the maximum surprise was achieved and the British had only small losses. Thirty guns, 300 jingals and 2,000 muskets were captured.

The defeat must have been a tremendous shock to Bundula's military pride, but far from giving up, he spent the next day, 6 December, rallying the defeated troops and using them to reinforce his line threatening the Great Pagoda, which was still within musket shot of the British positions. Campbell planned another heavy blow there next day and meantime to lull Bundula into a mistaken sense of security stopped all artillery fire and concealed his infantry, at the same time quietly reinforcing the position with heavy guns from the ships. Thus enticed, Bundula's troops advanced their trenches nearer and nearer, until the British heard their loud defiant hurrahs.

Mahâ Bundula in Command

For some reason Campbell did not start his attack next day until 11.45 a.m., when the guns until noon hammered the Burmese trenches with a heavy cannonade, which the Burmese returned with light guns, jingals and muskets. Four columns of British troops then advanced, one left, one right, and two centre, the latter two descending the stairs from the Pagoda's north gate. 'It was not until a decided charge was made,' Snodgrass noted, 'and our troops actually in the trenches that the enemy finally gave way: their courage failed them at this extremity, and they were precipitately driven from their numerous works ... into the thick forest in their rear ...

'Upon the ground the enemy left a great number of dead, who seemed generally, from their stout and athletic forms, to have been their best troops. Their bodies had each a charm of some description, in which the brave deceased had no doubt trusted for protection against all harm and every danger ...'

Bundula's defeat was completed by an attack next day upon his gun batteries on the far bank of the river at Dalla. It was so dark a night that the British, rowed over by the sailors with muffled oars, landed unobserved. They then marched in strict silence through the clumps of rustling bamboo towards the Burmese and, surprising them, after a little desperate bayonet fighting drove them off and took the position again with all its guns and stores.

Bundula, it seemed, had had enough, for that night, 7 December, he silently withdrew his troops from Kemmendine as well, taking with him almost all his dead, all his wounded and his equipment. 'Save a dead body here and there, the embers of their last night's fires,' wrote Ensign Doveton, who had gone there from Rangoon, 'and the appearance of the trees and shrubs that had been cruelly mutilated by our showers of shot, there was little of interest ... for the foe had taken special care to leave behind nothing that we could possibly convert into a trophy ...'

Thus, in the course of a few days Bundula, who had promised King Bagyidaw that within a week he would have driven the rebel foreigners into the sea or have captured them, was humbled beyond Burmese belief. The myth of invincibility was shattered.

The Burma Wars

Large-scale desertions followed while he was retreating north with the fear of the king's anger large in his mind. How total was the Burmese collapse the British losses of only 30 killed and 220 wounded from 1 to 9 December are evidence. Burmese losses in the same period were estimated to be at least 5,000 men, though they were probably rather less.

Campbell now believed that he had defeated Bundula finally and he was probably looking forward to a more or less unhindered march up the line of the Irrawaddy to King Bagyidaw's Court at Ava. But he was gravely mistaken.

On the evening of 12 December a Burmese deserter found his way into the British lines. Taken before Campbell, he swore that Bundula had received reinforcements during his retreat, which made him decide to try to retrieve his disgrace by another desperate effort. He had therefore returned to Kokeen, a village some four miles north of the Shwedagon, which a Burmese reserve corps had already begun to stockade along a high ridge commanding the road to Sanubyu.

Also, the deserter assured Campbell, it was Bundula's intention to attack the British on the morning of 14 December. They were determined to sacrifice their lives at the dearest rate, 'as they had nothing else to expect than to do so ignominiously by returning disgraced and defeated to the presence of their monarch ...'[3]

Campbell determined to take this information seriously and attack Bundula himself, at the right time. Meanwhile, the Burmese general, with a force of only about 25,000 men, began strengthening Kokeen's stockades and fortifications with solid trunks of teak. Around it he had dug a broad deep ditch sown thickly with bamboo stakes, as sharp as knives.

At the same time he embarked upon a stratagem to try to destroy all the military stores the British had accumulated in Rangoon. After his defeat, thousands of deserters and their families had entered the town, with British permission. Among them Bundula sent in his own fifth column, charged with this task. To mislead the British about his plans he caused a rumour to be spread that an envoy, a chief named Mounshoezar, had arrived at his headquarters from Ava with authority to negotiate

Mahâ Bundula in Command

peace. 'Our situation became critical in the extreme,' noted Snodgrass, who was always at Campbell's elbow.

> Spies, assassins and incendiaries lurked in every corner of Rangoon; every native within our lines became an object of suspicion and the utmost vigilance of the troops, combined with the energy and decision of their commander, could alone have prevented our losing every advantage of our late successes, by the destruction of our stores and magazines ... The inflammable materials of which the town was composed required but a single fire-brand to envelope [sic] our cantonments and everything they contained in a general conflagration; while the unseen enemy, lurking in the outskirts of the jungle, were held in constant readiness to rush in upon our lines during the confusion ...

These fears were justified. At midnight on 12 December fire broke out in several places at once in windward parts of the town. Helped by a high wind the flames swept through the thatch and bamboo houses with extraordinary violence until it looked as though they would reach the ammunition and stores depot in an adjoining area.

Expecting the Burmese to make a lightning attack during the confusion, Campbell ordered the drums to beat to arms for picquets to man the defence. At the same time companies of men ran off at the double through the surging smoke and the showers of sparks to try to stop the blaze reaching the danger area.

Exactly how this was done – by a human chain of water buckets, by thousands of men beating out the flames or destroying the flimsy houses and removing all timber from the fire's path – not even the meticulous Snodgrass reported, but after two hours, the flames were 'completely got under', with only slight damage to military property – and the destruction of a quarter of the town.

Surveying the smoking ruins – evidence of Bundula's power – next day, Campbell determined to undertake the risky task of sending a force through the jungle to Kokeen after him as soon as possible, which was two days later, 15 December. He

The Burma Wars

must have realised that the time had come for him to regain the initiative, despite the risks.

They were considerable for, first, with their numerical superiority, excellent sources of information and perfect knowledge of the jungle, the Burmese might overcome Rangoon while many of his troops were away assailing the Kokeen stockade. Secondly, he would have to march this force through the winding jungle footpaths where the Burmese snipers, from trees and thicket, could knock out hundreds of his men long before he reached Bundula's stronghold. Finally, he would have to order his troops to attack without artillery a fieldwork stronger than any they had yet faced, for they could take only one or two light guns.

But he had no choice, and early on 15 December, having left about 3,000 men to hold Rangoon and the Shwedagon he moved out against Bundula in two columns, the right of 540 men, British and Indian, under Brigadier-General Cotton, and the left, 800 strong, under his personal command. Cotton's force was to make a detour and attack from the rear, while Campbell's took them from the front. Surprisingly, Bundula's troops made not one attack on them during their short march north.

The Burmese position was of great strength, made up of two large stockades on either flank connected by a central trench. Each wing was some 400 yards long by 200 broad, and projected far beyond the centre. It was found to be defended by about 20,000 men. Campbell later reported that Bundula had thus shown 'a judgement in point of position such as would do credit to the best-instructed engineers of the most civilised and warlike nations'. As for the reaction of the British troops, Snodgrass noted grimly that 'they well knew there was no retreating, and that no choice was left between victory and an honourable grave.'

On emerging from the jungle they were met by a hail of rounds from hidden positions in nearby trees. At once Campbell ordered the signal guns to be fired to warn Cotton that he was about to attack, and hearing the reply while his men were deploying he launched the assault in two columns, one against each wing, while Cotton's force escaladed the high stockade

Mahâ Bundula in Command

walls with practised skill, drove back the enemy with disciplined volleys then went in with the bayonet. Cotton's division, especially HM's 13th, suffered heavy losses while exposed to the enemy's fire when storming several entrenchments in front of the main work. Finally, it too burst in and after some twenty minutes' close fighting the Burmese defenders dropped their arms and fled into the jungle.

Snodgrass was there to take careful note of the scene. 'The interior of the stockade, as well as the ditch,' he observed, 'were strewed with dead and dying, and many of the enemy, who found escape impossible, with the never-failing cunning and ingenuity of their nation, besmeared themselves with blood, and lay down under the dead bodies of their comrades, in the hope of escaping when darkness set in, but they were mostly discovered, and made prisoners.'

It was a quick victory, but the British paid dearly for it, in relatively heavy losses of 136 killed or wounded, the 13th regiment alone losing 11 officers and 51 men. The navy's always active Lieutenant Kellett, on board the *Diana* steamboat, had attacked the enemy's war-boat flotilla nearby during the fighting and by clever tactics captured 30 boats, including one gilt one mounting three guns, and destroyed many others, numbers of them loaded with ammunition and food for Bundula's forces.

These successive defeats of Bundula's troops before Rangoon changed the entire trend of the war, in so far as they crushed, for the time being at least, the Burmese hope of driving the 'rebel foreigners' from Rangoon and destroying their army. Bundula's shrunken forces retreated to Danubyu and he merely placed troops on the Hlaing and Panhlaing rivers to slow down the enemy advance. This coincided with the arrival of land and water transport for the British. So now that the way seemed open Campbell prepared to advance north and dictate peace terms within King Bagyidaw's 'golden city' of Ava.

7
Victory in the Balance

Everything improved for the British after Bundula's retreat from the Rangoon area. Burmese men, women and children, many exhausted and half-starved by unceasing forced labour on stockades, with little to eat except wild plants, straggled back into Rangoon from the jungle by the thousand every day. They willingly exchanged their own authorities' ferocity, which included capital punishment for even trivial offences, for the wild foreigners' decency and goodwill – and despite all its detractors, British rule did replace harsh tyranny by benevolent paternalism, a not inappropriate system for the day.

Never a race to lament for long, the Burmese set to work energetically to rebuild their charred homes and take up their trades. Remarkably soon, Rangoon came to life again. Its merchants opened a bazaar, and soon venison, fish, fruit and vegetables on sale there improved the army's diet. Beef the Buddhist religion forbade the Burmese to sell, but they had no objections to the sale of beef on the hoof. Many Burmese enlisted as drivers for the army's supply department wagons, which, with 1,700 draught oxen, had arrived from India. Boatmen too came forward, though not enough of them until the good pay and friendly treatment proved an attraction.

A steady flow of shipping from Calcutta and Madras with

provisions and reinforcements gave the campaign new zest. The British were cheered by the arrival of HM's 47th two squadrons of horse artillery, two of cavalry and a rocket troop, evidence that, far from being forgotten, the campaign was meant to be fought to a finish quickly. Campbell still hoped that the final dispersal soon of the Burmese forces at Danubyu might persuade King Bagyidaw and his counsellors to sue for peace. In January the delta country over which the army would have to march to reach the Irrawaddy and Danubyu was still too wet for the movement of artillery, even with the oxen teams now ready. Campbell decided that they should advance by 10 February and if peace did not follow a victory at Danubyu, in the short season before the next rains, they should be able to reach Prome, over 200 miles north and about a third of the way to Ava.

A force of 3,000 local troops under the tough Lieutenant-Colonel Richards had since October been driving the remaining Burmese units out of Assam, in the north, whence they had not long ago threatened India. In high rugged country, the campaign there was exhausting, but a team of ambitious and energetic young British officers under Richards had completed the task and except for tribesmen's occasional raids into the province, by the end of January India's north-eastern frontier was secured.

It was no less important to secure the eastern coast of the Bay of Bengal, mainly Arakan, and for this purpose was assembled a force of 11,000 including four British regiments,[1] commanded by Brigadier-General Morrison and aided by a naval force which included some 80 small gunboats. After conquering Arakan, it was expected that Morrison would be able to follow in the footsteps of Bundula's army and cross the formidable mountain range, the Arakan Yomas, into the Irrawaddy valley, and there link up with General Campbell. No less ambitious, a force of 7,000 under Brigadier Shuldham, had been assembled on the Sylhet frontier with the task of marching through Cachar and Manipur, then turning left and threatening Ava from the north.

In face of the rout of Bundula's forces that Campbell's army had achieved, it would seem that the British were now blindly over-doing it, faced at the same time by very sketchy knowledge

Victory in the Balance

of both climate and terrain. And these were the real enemies. Shuldham, struggling with heavy artillery and long ponderous columns of red-coated infantry up and down the ridges of forested mountains which continually crossed his road, floundering through mile after mile of deep mud worsened by heavy February rains, losing camels and elephants by the hundred in trying to keep his roadmakers and advance guards in provisions, had to give up by the end of March and report to Calcutta upon the campaign's impracticability.

Then occurred an event which underlines the power of knowledge of terrain and of simplicity in military operations. The Rajah of Manipur, dethroned by the Burmese, pleaded with Shuldham to be allowed to do the job himself with a mere 500 of his own men armed with British muskets and bayonets. Shuldham eventually agreed and the Rajah's force left Sylhet on 17 May, accompanied by Lieutenant Pemberton. After a hard march over the forested mountains in constant rainfall, they reached the western boundary of Manipur, with great difficulty, on 10 June. A Burmese garrison in Manipur town fled on their advance to a position about 10 miles south. When the Rajah and Pemberton advanced to attack for the second time the Burmese again withdrew. They were then driven from the province entirely. Leaving a number of troops and armed inhabitants to defend the town, if necessary, Pemberton and the Rajah returned to Sylhet, arriving on 22 June.

A few 'undisciplined mountaineers', as Wilson, the contemporary historian of the campaign calls them, had thus, at little expense, won this important campaign. Knowledge and simplicity — it was a lesson, to digress, which the Americans in Vietnam were slow to learn, nearly 150 years later. No echo of it informed General Morrison's campaign in Arakan in 1825 and the outcome was a military disaster. He marched along the new road south from Chittagong in January with his force of 11,000, heavy artillery and a supply line with camels, elephants and oxen that trailed behind for nearly fifteen miles.

At Cox's Bazaar, eight miles south of the ill-omened Ramu, ignorance of the terrain began to baffle him. Numerous creeks and rivers stretched between him and Arakan. He had to decide whether to follow the coast and transport his entire expedition across where the rivers had become wide estuaries; or to wheel east and cross them higher up where they were presumably easily fordable.

Morrison's problem was not knowing whether any usable tracks ran east, but he did know that he would face mountains and forests which his infantry might cross in reasonable weather, but not his artillery or the heavily loaded pack animals. So he chose the coast.

Fortunately, the British political agent had assembled large numbers of small boats, barges and rafts at Tek Naaf, about eight miles from the coast, where the river Naaf was some five miles wide. A detachment having crossed in them to Maungdaw and ascertained that there was no enemy and that the local people were friendly, Morrison ordered the entire force that had reached the bank by then to be ferried across. It was twelve days from 1 February to the 12, before it was safely over and ready to march on, but the baggage, stores, pack and beef cattle, camels and elephants were still on the other side, hundreds of them not yet having reached the river.

Worse was to come. Morrison left a senior officer with two squadrons of cavalry and two batteries of guns at Maungdaw to protect the rest of the crossing, while he divided his force into two, one to go by sea and the other by land, for the next stage, to Mayo. The land column reached its destination by 22 February, but the one at sea met with a violent storm which sank some of the freight boats and forced the others to put back to shore. Eventually, it arrived on 27 February and in this complicated way the entire force, except for nearly all its pack animals, was assembled at the mouth of the great Arakan river ready to march on by 24 March.

More similar problems faced Morrison, but the climate at this time was favourable, the troops were in good shape and supplies were plentiful. By 1 April he had taken Arakan city, in the fighting for which he lost only 23 killed and about 177 wounded. He then sent Brigadier-General Macbean south by water to occupy Ramree Island and Sandoway, on the coast lower down, where there was no resistance.

Victory in the Balance

Morrison had thus effectively taken possession of Arakan; and this should perhaps have been enough, but the Commander-in-Chief and the Governor-General in distant Calcutta wanted his entire army now to march over the Yoma mountains to link up with Campbell, on the Irrawaddy. It was the most formidable task of all and the prospect of it with the rains approaching must have shaken even the unflinching Morrison. First, between Arakan city and the foothills of the Yomas lay eighty miles of steaming jungle, then another ninety miles of rugged mountains and precipices across which guns, elephants and camels could be taken only with enormous difficulty, and at a very slow pace.

Sensibly, Morrison formed a reconnaissance column of six companies of British and Sepoy infantry, commanded by Major Bucke, and shipped them some eighty miles south to Dalek with orders to march thence to Talek and reconnoitre the Talek Pass, instead of, for some reason, the Aeng Pass, which was the normal trade route between Burma and Arakan.

On 19 May Bucke and his small force made their first tiring march up a steep, narrow and stony track. Then up a stony path, mostly wide enough for only one man, they climbed for the next three days. By the evening of the third day many of both British and Sepoys were either sick or exhausted, while those of their pack animals which had not tumbled down the mountainsides were too weak to go any farther.

They were now within two days' march of the Burmese frontier. For Bucke, high up among these windy wastes, it must have seemed that the prize was within his grasp, but it was to be snatched away. News came in on the 23rd through his native scouts that a hostile post lay ahead. Bucke made plans to overcome it with a night attack, but shortly before it the scouts returned with the news that a strong enemy force straddled the road a few miles ahead; two of his guides had been shot and two made prisoner.

Bucke's small force was in no shape to embark on what could well turn out to be a long and hard fight. He prudently decided to retreat and quickly put as many miles as he could between his troops and the Burmese. Further misfortune now caught up with him. On the plain the rains had already begun, and malaria with it. Before Bucke rejoined Morrison the majority of his men had caught what seems to have been a virulent form of it and had died.

Morrison and his troops in Arakan were no better off. Malaria and dysentery had struck them and the climate worsened the incidence. During July and August 103 inches of rain were measured, while often the temperature fell quickly from 92 to 78 degrees Fahrenheit and then up again.

The troops, imprisoned in bamboo huts with nothing to do in the steaming tropical heat but drink rum or arak, took to drunkenness, which, inevitably, made their condition worse. Dysentery and malaria reached epidemic proportions and up to the end of September, when all but small garrisons in the healthier Cheduba and Ramree Islands, and Sandoway, were withdrawn, 600 British troops out of about 1,500 had died and 900 Sepoys out of a total of 8,000. Some 400 British and 3,600 Sepoys were in hospital. Morrison contracted malaria and was invalided home to England, but died on the voyage.

Such was the outcome of the Government of India's blind ordering of the army into this unknown tropical hell.

Upon Campbell alone now rested the heavy task of bringing the campaign to a victorious end. Mahâ Bundula, apparently much affected by the disgrace of his defeat at Rangoon, had concentrated a fairly substantial force at Danubyu, which was already strongly fortified. Campbell had first to overcome this before beginning his advance north in two columns, one by water and the other by land. Had he possessed enough transport animals he might instead have advanced upon the capital by the shortest and best road, through Pegu and Toungoo, which would have enabled him, as well, to turn all the Burmese positions on the Irrawaddy; but for supply he was in every way dependent upon the river, so it was impossible. The plan he adopted, however, made no allowance for the defence of the parallel valley of the Sittang. Britain's allies, the Siamese, were therefore requested to advance upon Toungoo, though it was unlikely that they would do so.

Victory in the Balance

Under his personal command, Campbell took the land column, made up of 1,300 British infantry, a thousand Sepoys, two cavalry squadrons, a troop of horse artillery and the rocket troop. Twelve to fifteen days' provisions for this force was the most the available pack and wagon transport could carry, and this only by cutting out those small food and drink luxuries to which in India officers and men were accustomed. (Sometimes these were considerable. An officer in Afghanistan in 1840 confessed that his regimental mess had two camel loads of the finest Manilla cigars!)

Campbell's force was to advance parallel to the Hlaing river and then follow the Irrawaddy, linking up with the river-borne column before it reached Danubyu. Commanded by Brigadier-General Willoughby Cotton, this consisted of 800 British infantry, a small battalion of Sepoys and powerful batteries of heavy artillery, carried in a flotilla of 60 boats. Captain Alexander, RN, commanded these, escorted by the men-of-war *Satellite*, *Diana*, and the *Prince of Wales* and a number of smaller craft. A third force, which Major Sale commanded, was to sail by sea for Bassein, about 100 miles west of Rangoon, take possession of it then, leaving a small garrison, try to assemble enough land transport to cross north-east some sixty miles of swampy delta country to Danubyu.

Campbell's column moved off on 11 February with high hopes that at last they were about to subjugate an empire. They reached Hlaing without incident, and re-loaded the provision wagons from the boats which had followed up river. But instead now of turning west, as arranged, so as to reach the Irrawaddy below Danubyu to meet Cotton, Campbell went on north and passing east of Danubyu eventually reached the river nearly fifty miles above it at Tharrawaw on 2 March. From here he intended to march on a hundred miles to Prome, expecting to be joined somewhere en route by Cotton and the river column.

Cotton had meantime moved slowly up the Hlaing and Panhlaing rivers, meeting hostile forces here and there, capturing a big stockade at Panhlaing village after a sharp encounter and reaching the junction with the Irrawaddy on 27 February. Here the heavier ships grounded in the shallows; the *Diana* and the

The Burma Wars

gunboats had to be unloaded. While troops and navy were doing this, a fleet of Burmese war-boats attacked them, but were driven off, while two companies of the 89th Regiment landed and drove the enemy from an outpost, killing several of them and bringing in a prisoner. It was 5 March before the last of the fleet entered the Irrawaddy; the next day it took up a position about two miles below the white pagoda of Danubyu.

That morning General Cotton and Captain Alexander together reconnoitred a succession of formidable stockades which began at the white pagoda and increased in strength up to the main work, a teak and bamboo stockade 17 feet high surrounding the town's brick walls and linked to it by cross beams. It stretched 1,000 yards along the river bank and extended some 600 yards inland, forming a rough oblong. In front of it was a ditch 18 feet wide by 8 deep, in front of the ditch a tall bamboo fence, then a space of 18 feet sown with sharp spikes, another fence, an abattis then a final fence. The 40-foot-high river bank also formed a good defence and numerous garrison was seen behind these fortifications.

At 1.30 p.m. Cotton sent with a flag of truce a summons to Bundula to surrender, giving an hour for reply. A polite refusal to agree to the terms came at half-past three and Cotton gave the order to attack.

Campbell, during the last four days, had been waiting with growing anxiety for the sight of Cotton's flotilla rounding the bend of the great 800-yards-wide river below Tharrawaw. He had reloaded his wagons from the supply boats on 1 March, but it was for the last time; henceforward he depended upon Cotton's flotilla for provisions and ammunition, so without it the advance on to Prome was impossible. But his wagons carried supplies for fifteen days only; every day's waiting bore heavily on them, which added to Campbell's sense of frustration and increased his anxiety to advance.

Early on 7 March the welcome sound of a heavy cannonade echoed up the river valley from the south, lasting until 2 p.m. when it ended. Later, Burmese peasants came in with welcome reports that Bundula had been totally defeated down at

British forces built a stockade around their camp after the capture of Martaban in April 1852.
The *Illustrated London News* (March 1853)

British warships bombard Rangoon on Easter Sunday, April 1852, before landing the next day.
The Illustrated London News (June 1853)

An artist's impression of the British naval attack on the Dunnoo stockade in the Second Burmese War.
The National Maritime Museum

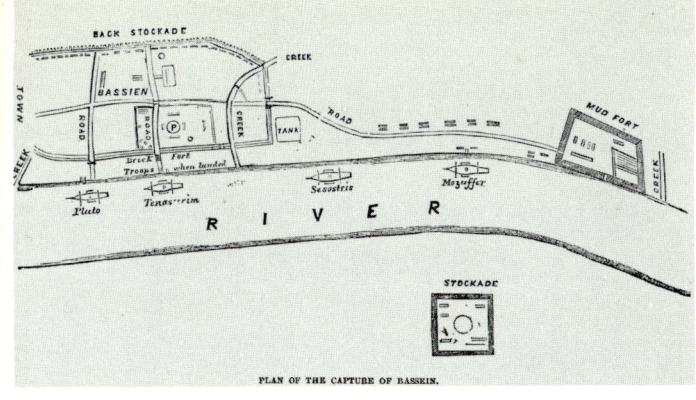

Plan of the capture of Bassein.
The Illustrated London News (July 1852)

A Royal Navy steam-ship squadron sails from Bombay for Rangoon. Technology had leapt forward since the first war in Burma.
The Illustrated London News (April 1852)

An artist's impression of the Rangoon stockades stormed by General Godwin's troops in April 1852.
The Illustrated London News (March 1852)

Advancing British troops of the British 18th and 80th regiments drive the enemy before them as they storm the Shwedagon Pagoda, Rangoon, April 1852.
The National Army Museum

British sailors pose before the Shwedagon Pagoda, Rangoon. This picture, taken by the pioneer photographer John MacCosh, shows the detail of the gilded teak carving.
The National Army Museum

The gate of the Shwe'dagon Pagoda, Rangoon 1853, taken from a contemporary sketchbook. This Great Pagoda was a fortress as well as a temple.
The National Army Museum

Part of the Rangoon stockade which was stormed by the British troops in the Second Burmese War, 1852. As drawn in an officer's sketchbook.
The National Army Museum

An officer's billet at Rangoon. This drawing shows a quite comfortable room, with mosquito net, sword, clock and baggage.
The National Army Museum

Victory in the Balance

Danubyu. Joyfully, Campbell accepted them as true – could the outcome, he must have reasoned, have been otherwise, in view of his past victories? He saw an immediate advance to Prome as imperative now so as to occupy it before the arrival of Bundula's defeated army, as well as to seize the cattle and rice said to be available there before the Burmese destroyed everything.

Prudently, however, he waited one more day, then on 9 March, with reports arriving of Bundula's hasty retreat, began his advance northwards once more, leaving a strong detachment behind to delay the retreating Burmese. For two days, past deserted and ruined villages he marched north through the jungle at the rate of about twelve miles a day, as far as the large town of U-au-deet, upon the right bank of the Irrawaddy. 'We found it wholly deserted,' noted Snodgrass, 'and every article that could be of use to us carried away.... The desertion of the towns and villages was obviously a systematical arrangement of the Burmhan chiefs.... Here we heard for the first time, that the King had ordered a house to be built for himself at Prome; and had given out that if the English continued their audacious march upon his capital there he would in person meet them, and give them signal cause to repent such rash proceedings.' If this caused laughter, the scorched earth policy did not, for no food whatever was to be had from the country and Campbell possessed on 11 March a mere ten days' provisions.

Soon after first light that day a messenger with a report from Cotton caught up with him. The attack on Danubyu had failed and without large reinforcements it could not be carried. Campbell's and Cotton's forces were now separated by a powerful Burmese army in the stronghold of Danubyu.

Reconnaissance had shown General Cotton that he had not enough troops to sail up river and attack the main Danubyu stockade while at the same time maintaining communications with his depot at Panhlaing, upon which the success of the campaign depended. Sickness, and the several small detachments doing garrison duty, had decreased his British troops until there were only 600 out of the total of 750 ready for action. Moreover, Bundula's gunners had greatly improved; the fire from his batteries was accurate and commanded the river. He needed a stronger, rather than a weaker force.

Worse still, he had no choice but to land at the first of the stockades and then painstakingly attack them one by one. At sunrise on 7 March, some 500 British troops were landed a mile below the glimmering white pagoda and formed into two columns, supported by two 6-pounders and a rocket battery. 'Both columns were led with the utmost steadiness,' wrote Lieutenant John Marshall of the Royal Navy.

> As they advanced, the armed boats pulled in and cannonaded; while, at proper range, a steady fire was opened from the field-pieces and rocket-battery. This the enemy returned with a perseverance and spirit that had seldom been evinced by them; the gorges of the work attacked were narrow, and completely occupied by the gallant troops who were forcing an entrance, which, when made good, left the Burmese, who are reported to have been 3,000 strong, no alternative but a passage over their own formidable defences.
>
> They were overtaken in the last abattis, where they stood to fire, until closed upon by the troops inside, and checked by others who had run round outside in search of an entrance to the body of the work. The dead, the wounded, and the panic-struck, fell in one common heap, in and close upon the abattis; of the two latter, 280 were brought in prisoners; and the total loss of the enemy, in this affair, cannot be estimated at less than 450 men The assailants had about 20 killed and wounded.

Cotton gave his men a short rest then deployed for the attack on the next stockade, about 500 yards up river, bringing up for this purpose two more 6-pounders, four 5½-inch howitzers and more rockets. When these had cannonaded the enemy's defences enough to soften them up, Captain Rose led 200 men to the assault. The Burmese at once opened volleys of destructive musketry, which made the columns swerve to the right of the point of attack and into a ditch filled with spikes, under fire.

Victory in the Balance

All who showed themselves were knocked down. Rose, wounded once already, tried by example to rally his men, but fell by a second shot. Captain Cannon took his place and was at once killed. Casualties among the men were also heavy. When five officers and about a hundred men were seen, through the smoke that swirled around the ditch, to have fallen, Cotton called off the attack and the bugles sounded the peremptory notes of the retreat.

'Although I feel convinced that I could have carried the second work,' Cotton reported to Campbell, 'it would have been with a further loss, which would prevent an attempt on the main stockade, and I should have been either left in a position exposed to one of superior strength, or have to relinquish the post after carrying it at a great sacrifice.' So at 2 a.m. on 8 March he re-embarked his men, with all their guns and stores, and dropped down river to Youngyoun, ten miles below Danubyu, from where he had moved early on the 6th.

This defeat was the price Campbell had paid for leaving the burden of attacking Danubyu entirely upon Cotton's small force. He had no choice now but to fall back as quickly as possible, join Cotton before Danubyu and launch a second joint attack upon it.

With what fury he began the march back can be imagined, especially because Danubyu was on the west bank of the Irrawaddy, while he was on the east bank and had therefore somehow to ferry his entire army, with artillery and cavalry, across 800 yards of rapid water, with nothing but a few small canoes. But timber there was in plenty, rafts were quickly made and after the troops had worked day and night, every man had been ferried across by the 17th, five days later. Two more days, however, were taken up with reloading the transport wagons and not until 21 March was Campbell marching south, amid tall elephant grass nearly twenty feet high, through which his prisoners had cut a path.

Narrowly escaping being engulfed by a grass fire's flames on the 23rd, his troops marched another twelve miles next day to within four miles and easy sight of Danubyu's main stockade, from whence a fleet of war-boats came out and cannonaded one of his reconnoitring parties. The tall masts of Cotton's flotilla could be seen through the haze, near the horizon, lying at anchor in the 800-yards-wide river.

By 25 March Campbell was ready for action. He advanced with the intention of surrounding the entire main stockade, but finding it more than half a mile long on the river front, instead took up a position with his left wing on the river and his right curved round towards the centre of the stockade's western face, anchored on nothing more solid than an extensive bamboo thicket, whose long narrow leaves shone like bayonets.

That day, 25 March 1825, was a Friday, the seventh day of the Waxing of the Moon of the Month of Tabaung in the Burmese calendar,[2] and moonset would have been about 10 p.m. Shortly before this hour the Burmese liked to launch night attacks so that if forced to retreat they could do so in the dark, and knowing this the British had thrown out a strong picquet line.

Bundula had created a lookout tower in a giant tree within the stockade, with three heavy guns placed on high platforms at different levels. From it, he closely surveyed the British preparations and, noted Snodgrass, 'everything about the stockade bespoke system and judgement in the chief, with order, confidence and regularity in the garrison.'

Having seen from his perch in the tree the weakness of the British right flank, resting only on thin jungle, Bundula suddenly struck at this at about 9.30 p.m. The right flank picquet fired shots in warning then fell back to the main British position. Gongs beat, muskets fired and a full-throated roar came in unison from a large body of Burmese troops which had stalked from the rear of the main stockade and swept around to the northwest to outflank the British right.

HM's 38th and 26th Madras Light Infantry at once changed front to their right, knelt down to take better aim, and waiting until the charging Burmese were within thirty yards, knocked them down with heavy volleys in the glare from the flames of a hut the enemy had foolishly set alight. Gongs sounded again in the gloom, the enemy withdrew, then charged once more, but now the field artillery had come up to shower them with grape and cannister shot. Once again they retreated and again the gongs sounded for a fresh charge, but this time in vain. The regular and methodical volleys mowing down the foremost, the solid shot spinning through the column and the shriek and explosion of the rockets, were too deadly to be faced for long. The Burmese broke, fled and took refuge behind the walls of their fort. Soon all was quiet except for the nocturnal jungle sounds and the rest of the night passed without repetition of this desperate attack.

Once more, both sides in the conflict had witnessed the great gulf between Bundula's brilliant planning and his troops' inability to press home an attack successfully by means of disciplined advance in formation. Equipment apart, this was the main difference between the two armies – military discipline and organisation. It would prove decisive.

But Campbell had now to deal with the urgent problem of shortage of provisions and ammunition. Even on 10 March, Snodgrass reports, he was down to less than ten days' rations; it was now the 26th and he was still isolated from Cotton's force, with its abundant supplies. Presumably, he had put his troops on to half rations, for Bundula had seen to it that there was nothing left to eat in the countryside.

Campbell therefore sent a small column of 300 men around the western face of Danubyu to force its way through the uncleared jungle with the help of three elephants and take a message to Cotton to come up next day, which they succeeded in doing. Their return being opposed by Bundula, the troops joined Cotton's force and came up on board. Under heavy fire the flotilla approached the guns of the stockade in brilliant sunshine, led by the steamboat *Diana*. The navy's gunboats and brigs returned the enemy fire with precision, while Campbell's field artillery and howitzers in the camp at the same time assaulted the eastern ramparts and water batteries. Many of the Burmese guns were dismounted and their gunners killed. One British boat, holding the Madras European Regiment, was holed, but managed to reach the western bank without sinking.

Bundula saw clearly enough the danger for him of the British force uniting and did his utmost to prevent it. Burmese sources tell of him maintaining discipline by personally beheading two gunners who ran away when the British shot began to hiss

The Burma Wars

through the air, but he also encouraged his men by sighting guns on the river bank outside the stockade himself, under fierce fire. At the same time he organised a desperate sortie in force, for infantry, cavalry and seventeen caparisoned war elephants each carrying a number of troops armed with musket or jingal, suddenly assaulted Campbell's weak right flank, with flags flying, gongs beating and the Invulnerables out in front dancing, singing and waving their weapons aloft. The moment was well chosen, for the flotilla had passed the stockade and was then busy anchoring and could give no help.

Campbell, with foresight, had prepared for just such a situation. The horse artillery galloped forward in front of the camp and began a raking fire into the Burmese flank at about 500 yards' range. It caused havoc, knocking down the enemy in swathes, leaving heaps of dead and wounded, but with great courage the mass still charged the British right flank. Campbell ordered the dragoons of the Bodyguard to charge and they wove through the cumbersome lines of elephants, which thundered on until their riders were shot off their backs, whereupon they turned about and ambled back into the stockade with 'the greatest composure'. The entire Burmese force then realised the hopelessness of the task and retreated pell-mell into the fort. One can imagine the unfortunate Bundula's feelings of despair as this last chance of keeping the enemy forces split up failed, and with it his main chance of defeating them.

Campbell intended now to hammer Danubyu with his heaviest guns instead of trying to take it by storm, the preservation of his precious troops' lives being his first concern. The last three days of March were therefore spent constructing batteries and landing heavy guns from the flotilla. On 1 April he ordered his mortars and rockets to open up.

In salvoes the rockets hissed skyward and descended with ear-splitting combinations of explosions behind the enemy ramparts. These were lucky shots, for early nineteenth-century rockets had not been perfected and were at first not reliable. A salvo was fired when Campbell reconnoitred Danubyu on the day of his arrival; all of them exploded prematurely on the ground, shattering the tubes and scattering deadly fragments in

Victory in the Balance

all directions, but hurting no one. At Yandabo in February similar premature explosions occurred. Clumsy handling of these somewhat delicate weapons was the cause, and although the trouble was in due course largely overcome, defiant senior officers of the artillery nevertheless repudiated them and rockets were eventually discarded until more than 100 years later.

But throughout 1 April 1825 these and the mortars went on with their work of destruction. Wisely, the Burmese took cover and did little to return the enemy fire, much to the surprise of everyone. At daylight next day it was the turn of the breaching batteries and for some time the 18-pounders smashed their missiles against the teak defences, but there was still utter silence behind the splintered ramparts. Suddenly, two Bengali seamen, prisoners of the Burmese, came running out shouting desperately, during a pause in the firing. Bundula himself, they said, had been killed the day before by a rocket. And when this occurred in the full view of all, the soldiers had refused to stay and fight under any other commander, even the dead general's brother. During the night the entire garrison had fled silently into the jungle, leaving their arms and equipment behind them.

It was a lucky outcome indeed. One fortunate shot with the rockets despised by orthodox gunners had thus removed Bundula from the entire conflict and delivered Danubyu into Campbell's hands, together with huge supplies of grain, 130 guns and hundreds of other weapons.

Bundula, it was afterwards learned, had been overwhelmed by the disgrace of his defeat before the Great Pagoda. Afterwards he had looked for death and at Danubyu had sternly refused to take shelter during the British bombardment, or even order his attendant to lower his gilded state umbrella. He was reported to have said: 'If I die the enemy will attribute victory to that. They cannot say our soldiers were not brave.' Bluntly he told his officers at Danubyu that he would conquer or die and set his men the example of courage until he fell.

The news of Bundula's defeat and the dispersal of his army burst upon King Bagyidaw and his court at Ava like a bombshell. Bagyidaw heard the news in silent amazement and the queen beat her breast and cried, 'Ama! Ama!' (Alas! Alas!). Everyone asked who could lead the armies against the British now that the invincible Bundula was dead.[2] Bagyidaw and his ministers feared that the enemy would advance at once on the capital. A ripple of fear ran through the court.

Now the king began strongly to regret war with the British. He told John Christian, Portuguese chief of the palace artillery, who carried the king's sword, that he was 'in the predicament of a man who had got hold of a tiger by the tail, which it was neither safe to hold nor let go.'[3] He knew now that his troops were no match for the 'white strangers', and wished he had never started the war, but wounded pride and the palace astrologers' continued predictions of victory nevertheless made him continue. Fresh hopes were roused, men were levied for a new army in all parts of the empire, the arsenals were kept busy day and night manufacturing gunpowder, repairing old weapons and making new ones.

One of the king's ministers, the Pakan-Woon, who had been imprisoned for suspected treason, sent a message to Bagyidaw that he would lead the army, conquer the British and recover all the territory that they had seized. So desperate was Bagyidaw that he accepted the offer, released the Pakan-Woon and restored him to former eminence. At this person's suggestion, every soldier was to be given a generous sum at once. Against his better judgement the king agreed, but soon heard that the new general had kept most of this money for himself.

In the moral climate of the place and time, this was reasonable, hardly an event to overshadow the Pakan-Woon's future, but he then made two audacious and highly suspicious requests. First, that he should be allowed to take the Royal Bodyguard with him to battle: second, that Bagyidaw should leave the royal palace and go to the Mengoon Pagoda to pray and make offerings for military success. Both acts, if carried out, would effectively strip the king of power.

Bagyidaw easily saw through this clumsy scheme to make him leave the royal palace – occupation of which gave him his divine right as king – and also to strip him of his guard. He decided it was treason and ordered the Pakan-Woon to be

Victory in the Balance

seized, beaten through the city to the palace of execution and there trodden to death with elephants, which was done. Bagyidaw then transferred command of the new army to his brother the Prince of Tharrawaddy. About 70,000 strong, it was assembled at Meaday, forty miles north of Prome.

Meanwhile, Campbell had set his army in motion again, Cotton sailing up by the Irrawaddy towards the objective of Prome, while he himself rode at the head of the land column past the smoking ruins of villages and through the deserted countryside – for the Burmese, despite Bundula's death, still followed his policy of denying their enemy everything.

Then one morning Campbell received a letter from two of the king's advisers saying that Bagyidaw was ready to end the war by treaty. Campbell answered that he would be ready to negotiate after he had arrived in Prome. He received another letter saying that Prome should not be occupied, but that negotiations should be opened in the space of country between the Burmese and British armies. Campbell declared that the military occupation of Prome could not be dispensed with, and continued to advance. He finally entered it on 25 April, to find it mostly in flames behind a newly built line of defences and all the inhabitants driven into the jungle. The offer to negotiate, it seemed, had been simply a ruse to gain time.

Ava was still 200 miles north and to reach it before the rains came, in about two weeks, was impossible. Campbell therefore decided to put his army into quarters at Prome and the troops settled in as best they could. Soon the inhabitants began to return, houses were rebuilt, good relations were established between British and Burmese, civil magistrates were reinstated, with limitations on their authority; food appeared on the markets in abundance and the health of the troops was reasonably good. Only one man in seven died of dysentery, cholera or malaria during this period.

Campbell believed that after the rains he would at last be able to end the war quickly, either by military victory or by a treaty, on his own terms. During the long days and weeks of the monsoon when rain splashed down unceasingly from the low black clouds it was an encouragement for all.

8

Burmese Silver

Hopefully, in September, Campbell wrote to the Burmese command warning of the 'ruinous consequences' to the king of prolonging the war and urging them to listen to the lenient peace terms that he offered. In return, a mission from Ava arrived at Prome in due course to state the king's own desire for peace and the two sides therefore agreed that negotiations should open on the plain of Neoun-ben-zeik half way between Prome and Meaday. The Burmese, it was later discovered, had expected the British to march inflexibly upon Ava and regarded the offer to negotiate as evidence of weakness, perhaps of sickness among the troops. It naturally stiffened their attitude to the negotiations.

An armistice was arranged. The Kee Wungyi, or prime minister, and his party, afterwards camped on the plain a mile away from Sir Archibald Campbell and his aides, each group escorted by 600 men, the Kee Wungyi's rank not letting him move with a smaller escort. Both groups then left their camps at the same time and met at an equi-distant conference house where, after much hand shaking, demonstrations of friendly feelings and Burmese inquiries after the British royal family's health, the two parties sat down in chairs facing each other, and started talking.

The Burma Wars

But, Campbell's Military Secretary, Snodgrass, noted, 'it was too evident, from the very first, that the negotiations would lead to nothing.' Campbell stated the British terms – they included cession of Arakan and Tenasserim plus an indemnity of a million sterling – together with a recital of the war's causes. The Burmese listened, tried to persuade him to withdraw the main demands on the grounds that it might cost them their heads to tell Bagyidaw about them, and finally asked for another twenty days' armistice so that His Majesty's commands upon the issue might be received by them.

This Campbell granted; but within two or three days reports began to come in that Burmese army detachments had entered the neutral armistice zone burning, plundering and laying the country waste almost up to the gates of Prome, cutting off river-borne supplies for the army and threatened British communications with Rangoon and the sea.

Campbell sent strongly worded protests to the Kee Wungyi, who denied all knowledge of it. Finally, towards the end of the twenty days, he received a laconic answer to his terms: 'If you wish for peace, you may go away; but if you ask either money or territory, no friendship can exist between us. This is Burmhan custom!'[1]

The entire Burmese army, obeying the king's new commands to surround and attack the rebel strangers on all sides, then advanced upon Prome in three divisions. The one on the right, 15,000 men, crossed the Irrawaddy and moved forward so as to intercept British communication with their rear. The centre one, up to 30,000 strong and commanded personally by the Kee Wungyi, advanced down the east river bank, supported by a fleet of war-boats escorting the provision and supply vessels. More to the east, on the far side of a belt of forest, marched the left division, also 15,000 strong, commanded by Mahâ Nemiao, an old and experienced general lately arrived from the court with orders from Bagyidaw to direct the general operations of the army in what was thought to be a new style of warfare. How this was to be done when he was divided from the centre column by a forest barrier several miles thick, so that each column could be attacked separately without being able to aid the other, is hard to understand. But as well as these three corps, a reserve of 10,000 men occupied a strongly fortified position at Minhla; another force was ready to oppose any enemy advance from Arakan and still another in the region of old Pegu, threatened an attack on Rangoon.

Campbell's hopes of a swift finish seemed dashed, for altogether it added up to a formidable threat, considerably stronger on the face of it than the power with which the British could counter it. At Prome, Campbell had only six weak British battalions, making 2,800 of all ranks; seven battalions of the Madras Native Infantry, about 3,000, besides a troop of the Governor-General's Bodyguard and a strong force of foot and horse artillery. Rangoon was held merely by a garrison force of 3,000, mainly Sepoys; while at old Pegu were the 102nd Regiment and three Sepoy battalions. So that after garrisoning Prome, Campbell had a field force to meet the enemy north of it of some 5,000 men, just over half British. It was hardly enough.

Mahâ Nemiao, now putting into operation the new strategy which, it was hoped, would finally turn the tide against the British, advanced to Watty-goon, sixteen miles north-east of Prome, from where he threatened to cut Campbell's links with the south. Campbell therefore, on 15 November, sent Colonel McDowall and three battalions of Madras Native Infantry to attack the enemy's left flank while one battalion held them in front. But Mahâ Nemiao's scouts had told him of the British moves. In sharp contrast to the usual Burmese stockade tactics, he didn't wait to be attacked, but sent his troops out against the enemy and meeting them half way began a running fight through the jungle, aided by cavalry whenever open country intervened.

In this way he completely prevented the juncture of McDowall's forces. Two battalions of them reached the Watty-goon stockade separately, but both failed in their attack. McDowall was shot dead while reconnoitring it; a retreat was ordered. One column had to fight off jungle attacks through almost the whole sixteen miles. Total losses amounted to 12 officers and 188 men killed or wounded.

The Burma Wars

A discouraging start for Campbell, it emboldened the veteran Nemiao, who now advanced upon the British at Prome, prudently stockading every mile as he moved, while bringing forward at the same time the centre and the right column on the far side of the river. Soon the British saw the centre column from Prome stockading the heights of the ridge of Napadi, five miles distant. 'Every day now produced a change in the Burmese line, working incessantly, night and day,' Snodgrass noted.

> Each morning discovered to us some new work in front of where their advanced parties had been posted on the preceding evening. It seemed to be the intention of the veteran chief ... not to risk his reputation, and perhaps his head, by any rash attempt which might lead to failure, but to push his approaches so near that a simultaneous and overwhelming rush might be made from all sides upon the British force.... His astrologers had foretold that an approaching lunar eclipse would undoubtedly prove a favourable time for commencing his attack.

Eight thousand Shan troops from the hills of northern Burma who had not yet fought against the British and were expected to display some toughness had reinforced the Burmese army. They were encouraged by three young and beautiful Shan women of high social rank, prophetesses who, it was believed, possessed also the miraculous power of turning aside the enemy shot and shell. Attractive, in a sort of Amazonian dress, the three rode their ponies among the troops, predicting a speedy victory and urging them with vibrant voices to destroy the rebel strangers. Whether these women were part of the Burmese monarch's apparatus of deception, or had some ancient anthropological meaning it is hard to say.

Campbell and his staff saw clearly that the two Burmese divisions on the east of the river were so far apart that they could not give each other any support. This was positively playing into his hands, for he could now overcome each separately. On 1 December, Commodore Sir James Brisbane opened a heavy cannonade upon the enemy's western and centre columns, a feint to draw his attention while Campbell, leaving four regiments of Sepoys to hold Prome, formed two columns, one under his and the other under Cotton's command, to attack Mahâ Nemiao's division at Simbike. At the same time, as part of the feint, a force of Sepoys moved as if to attack the Kee Wungyi's position at Napadi.

Cotton's force marched straight along the road to Simbike; Campbell's, after fording the Nawin river, moved as quietly as possible along its bank so as to attack from the rear and cut off retreat upon the Kee Wungyi's division.

It was a complicated but clever plan and well executed, for the enemy picquets had been all withdrawn, probably sent in the direction of the harassed centre column, so that Nemiao's position at Simbike was exposed to a sudden attack. Cotton reached it first, divided his force into two parties and assaulted two different points of the enemy stockades. The Shans, urged on by old Mahâ Nemiao himself – carried from point to point in a gilded palanquin – fought well until the British forced their way over the stockade ramparts and advanced in line upon them with destructive volleys. 'Horses and men ran in wild confusion from side to side, trying to avoid the fatal fire,' Snodgrass observed. 'Groups were employed in breaking down and trying to force a passage through the defences, while the brave, who disdained to fly, still offered a feeble and ineffectual opposition to the advancing troops.'

Nemiao fell while still urging his men to stand their ground; his body, with sword and gold chain of office, was afterwards found among those of his attendants. One of the beautiful Shan fortune-tellers was found wounded in the breast and carried from the battleground to a nearby cottage, where in a short time she died. Campbell's column met the Burmese and Shan troops running from the stockade through the jungle, where the horse artillery opened up on them. A shrapnel shell exploded above another of the Shan ladies while she was crossing the river on horseback; she fell into the water and was carried off by her attendants.

The Burmese left division had thus been routed, the commanding general killed.

The Burma Wars

Campbell decided to attack the Kee Wungyi's centre column at dawn next day, to try and overwhelm it before he retreated. After allowing his troops two hours' rest he marched them back to a bivouac near the ford of the river Nawin. This they reached after dark, tired out after nearly fourteen hours' marching and fighting through jungle and forest in the stifling heat. During the night Campbell sent a message to Commodore Brisbane requesting him to be ready to move the flotilla forward to cannonade the enemy position at Napadi as soon as the troops moved out of the jungle to attack.

At dawn next day, 2 December, the long columns of redcoats were swallowed up by the ubiquitous jungle green after somehow having found the energy for another day's fighting in far harder country. Campbell's column took a jungle path which brought it out upon a dusty yellow plain below Napadi's stockaded heights; Cotton's tried to find a way through the forest behind Napadi to strike at the Burmese rear.

The Kee Wungyi, or his military advisers, had chosen what looked like an almost impregnable position. Ranges of hills rose in a bend of the Irrawaddy, the second commanding the first and the third the second, all lying between the river's green verge and the dark forest behind the topmost range. Along the flat sandy beach lay the only road to the heights, but this was exposed to the fire of Burmese troops stockaded in nearby jungle. Campbell ordered six companies of HM's 87th to make their way through the jungle, attack this stockade from the rear and drive out the enemy. And this, in a matter of two hours, they accomplished.

A line of masts could be seen in the distance as Commodore Brisbane sailed up river, cannonading both the Napadi heights and the Burmese positions on the western bank as well. As the echoes of the gunfire ceased rumbling along the heights Campbell began anxiously awaiting the sound of musketry which would signal Cotton's attack from the rear and give the frontal assault up those steep brown ridges a fair chance of succeeding.

But it was not to be: Campbell the optimist was frustrated again. He waited anxiously for what seems to have been three or four hours for Cotton's attack, then formed up his troops for the grim frontal assault alone, first ordering Colonel Elrington to take the 47th Foot and the 38th Madras Native Infantry through the jungle and make a diversionary attack upon the enemy's left flank. Sound tactics often saved Campbell when optimism led him to venture too far.

Elrington luckily succeeded soon in getting through the jungle and diverting Burmese attention from their front. Campbell then gave the word, and HM's 13th, 38th and 87th regiments slowly and deliberately began the uphill advance without returning a shot to the Burmese volleys and stormed the first two stockades at the base of the lowest hill. It was exhausting work, yet under a heavy fire in the burning heat they again marched steadily forward, conserving energy as best they could, clearing the stockades at the summit of the next range and finally routing the enemy on the third as well, thus mastering the entire position, some three miles in extent. 'The defeat of the enemy on the left bank of the Irrawaddy was now complete,' Snodgrass noted. 'Between 40 and 50 pieces of artillery were captured and the material of his army taken or destroyed: his loss, in killed and wounded, had been very severe; and by desertion alone he had lost at least a third of his men.'

During the assault, Commodore Brisbane and the naval flotilla captured 300 enemy boats, containing what seem to have been Burmese reserve stores of grain, shot, gunpowder and weapons.

After this feat of exceptional courage and endurance, which showed again that a feudal horde, even under the most favourable conditions, could not withstand the disciplined troops of an industrial power, the defeat of the third enemy division on the far side of the river was soon done. Campbell set up rocket and mortar batteries on an island within range of the enemy stockades, pounded them for two or three hours early on 5 December, then landed infantry higher up who attacked their left flank and rear. After their defeats on the far side, the Burmese put up a very weak resistance and were driven from both stockades with substantial losses.

These three actions were a turning point in the war. For the Burmese, who made no more offensive movements and thereafter retreated northwards to link up with their reserves; and for the

The Burma Wars

British, who now believed they saw victory for certain within their grasp.

But the implacable Campbell gave his army only two or three days' rest; then deployed the weary troops for the march north towards the distant capital, once more in two divisions, Cotton with a track parallel to the river in communication with the flotilla; his own three days in advance and to the right. Enemy reserves under Prince Memiaboo were known to be at Meaday, sixty miles north on the Irrawaddy.

Campbell therefore intended to turn this and other enemy positions by a wide flanking movement, linking up with Cotton there. He also believed that Brigadier Morrison would come over the mountains from Arakan, and Richards too, from Assam, to join him, being unaware of the sad outcome of these two campaigns. So he was moving alone into the depths of this strange and unpredictable country.

Provisions for two months, mainly rice and biscuit in ox-drawn wagons, accompanied the six-mile-long procession of infantry in their torn and muddy red coats and barely recognisable white trousers. Heavy rains deluged the jungle paths on 11 and 12 December, officers and men stumbled forward through dripping 20-foot-high elephant grass, the ground became a yellow morass, wagons and artillery were bogged down, and soon exhausted or dead transport animals and their loads blocked the way. After a night spent in a dried-up river bed, the troops were again hit by cholera on 13 December, which killed quickly scores of both Sepoy and British before it abated.

Evidence of the enemy's scorched earth policy was first seen at Seindoop, formerly a large town and then a heap of ashes, deserted but for starving cats and dogs.

Campbell was joined, according to plan, a few miles before Meaday on 18 December, by Cotton's division, which brought with it more cholera. Next day, Campbell entered Meaday and perhaps for the first time realised how bitter and implacable was the determination of the Burmese chiefs to deny him everything the country had in abundance, from animals and food to friendly people and shelter. Dead and dying enemy soldiers covered the ground inside and outside the stockades, victims

Burmese Silver

of wounds, disease and starvation: among them were villagers driven from their homes and smallholdings, and left to starve alone.

Soldiers who had followed their chiefs' example in flying from the advancing British, or those who had left their posts in search of food, perhaps, were found grimly crucified – tied hand and foot to a diagonal cross of bamboo, a splinter forced through their tongues to keep their mouths open and then left to the voracious attacks of ants, flies and the packs of dogs and vultures that growled and screamed in fights to glut themselves.

In this nightmare atmosphere, with its appalling stench, the army spent the night, then at dawn next day marched on a few miles, but the Burmese dead had first to be removed from jungle clearings used as camping grounds, while patrols reported that for 50 miles ahead villages had been razed, people and cattle driven off, so that a once populous region had become a desert.

On 20 December the supply of the essential beef for the British troops failed to arrive. Campbell therefore ordered them to rest where they were until the supply wagons came up and marched on himself with the vegetarian Sepoys of the Indian regiments. 'Not a head of cattle, or indeed, a living thing, except the sick and dying stragglers from the Burmese army, was met with on the march,' Snodgrass observed.

> We appeared to traverse a vast wilderness from which mankind had fled; and our little camp of two thousand men seemed but a speck in the desolate and dreary waste that surrounded it, calling forth at times, an irksome feeling which could be with difficulty repressed, at the situation of a handful of men in the heart of an extensive empire, pushing boldly forward to the capital, still 300 miles distant; in defiance of an enemy whose force still outnumbered ours in a tenfold ratio, and without a hope of further reinforcement from our distant ships and depots.

On 27 December, when his column had doggedly marched forward another ten miles, envoys with a white flag of truce brought in letters telling of the arrival in Minhla nearby of

The Burma Wars

negotiators sent by Bagyidaw with powers to conclude a peace treaty. But after two officers had held talks with them Campbell decided it was merely a ruse to gain time, so having been then joined by the flotilla, he broke off the talks and advanced to Patanago, facing Minhla, which lay on the river's opposite, or western bank.

The army had now marched 140 miles from Prome, and so effectually had the Burmese succeeded in laying waste the line of the advance that the British had not met one man or woman on their feet along the river's normally thickly peopled banks; or been able to obtain one day's meat from a country generally thick with cattle.

Campbell would now have been asking himself with real anxiety if Bagyidaw intended to continue this policy beyond Ava, his capital, to the country's most northerly boundaries. For if he were to do so British military victories would prove fruitless, the army's supplies would eventually fail and his troops would face starvation. A grim and threatening prospect of defeat lay ahead.

So he pressed on fast. Speedy reconnaissance of Minhla revealed a vast stockade about two miles long on the river front and half a mile in depth. A tall gilded pagoda rose up in the interior, later found to be a memorial to Bundula raised by the king. Burmese troops still worked on the defences, the muzzles of brass guns shone along the ramparts, while beneath them at anchor on the glassy brown water, lay a large fleet of war-canoes.

Soon the flotilla arrived, and led by the steamboat *Diana* passed close by the enemy's stockade – without a shot being fired against it. Then, surprisingly, two gilt war-canoes received the *Diana* with paddles raised in salute and escorted it to an anchorage a little higher up river, which commanded any likely Burmese retreat by water.

Campbell took this courtesy as evidence of a Burmese wish to avoid more fighting. During the afternoon he agreed on a truce and arranged to start negotiating a treaty the next day. Peace, and the end of his anxieties, now seemed actually within grasp. It was a time for optimism. 'I sincerely hope,' he wrote on

31 December, 'that this is the last military despatch I shall have to write upon the war in Ava.'

The two sides met, next day, in a large vessel with shady awnings moored in mid-river between the two armies. The Kee Wunghi, prime minister; the Kolein Menghi, who was the king's deputy, and a number of chiefs represented the Burmese. Campbell was accompanied by General Cotton, Commodore Brisbane, Snodgrass and other staff officers. 'After the parties were seated in the boat,' Snodgrass noted, 'Kolein Menghi's mouth continued for some time so full of pawn-leaves and betel-nut ... as to prevent him from uttering a word distinctly, while the overflowing of the delicious juice ran in greenish-yellow streams down his chin, until checked and absorbed in the long tuft of hair which all Burmese chiefs wear as a mark of distinction.'

The British terms had been given to the Burmese during the earlier treaty discussions at Prome. They included the cession of Arakan and Tenasserim provinces for ever, to the British Government; agreement by the King of Ava to renounce all right of interference with Assam, Cachar and Manipur, and to recognise the reinstatement of the former Rajah of Manipur if that chief desired it. Finally, the king was to pay to the British an indemnity of one crore of rupees, which amounted to the enormous sum of one million sterling.

So the Burmese were to lose almost their entire sea coast, as well as to hand over a sum worth today about a hundred million sterling.

These, and the treaty's other demands and articles, urged the Burmese envoys into stubborn arguments, in which the Kolein Minghi, as the king's deputy, played the leading part. At first his opposition to paying the indemnity was academic. 'In war the expense is not all on one side,' Snodgrass quotes him as arguing:

We also have expended immense sums, leaving our treasury at the present moment drained and exhausted; it is evident, indeed, that our expenses must have greatly exceeded yours, as we have had to raise and appoint four or five new armies, one after another, and have had at all times since you came to the country, an immense multitude eating the public bread, and receiving the King's money, a great part of whose revenue has been stopped; while you, by means of discipline, and good management, have never required a large force, nor had above a small body of men to pay and provide for.

When told that every English soldier cost the Government nearly £200 before he reached his present situation and that every one of the many ships that came to Rangoon also cost an immense sum, he declared:

I also have been a merchant, and engaged in extensive mercantile transactions, but none of my vessels ever cost anything like the sum you mention, but whether or not, it is cruel to exact a sum which we cannot pay; our forests contain fine trees, you may cut them down; we could, perhaps, with economy, in one year, give you a million baskets of rice; but we do not grow rupees, and have in no way the means of procuring such a sum as you require.

King Bagyidaw's deputy, an inflexible and tenacious negotiator, was still more eloquent over the issue of territory. 'We are stingy of parting with Arakan, not for its value but because the honour of the nation is, in some measure, concerned in its retention,' the industrious Snodgrass quotes him as saying:

The people still look back with pride and exultation to its conquest, and they would regard its cession as robbing their forefathers, who achieved its subjugation, of their fame and glory. It has been for a long series of years in our possession; its native princes live in comfort and in honour at our capital, and its whole revenue scarcely suffices to discharge the expenses it incurs. Still, we would wish to keep the province, and would rather that you asked something in its room.

With regard to Cassay, it is a barren desert, and of little

use to us: our King sent troops into the country, at the request of the proper Rajah, who solicited protection, as a vassal, against a faction that was formed against him: our troops expelled the refractory chiefs from Munnipoore, and the Rajah now resides at Ava: he, and not Gumbheer Sing, is the legitimate Prince of Cassay; he prefers living at our court: but if you wish his country to be independent, he is the person who should be appointed king.[2]

For three days the haggling went on, the Burmese envoys defending, no less than in war, the country's territorial and monetary independence. Finally, they had no alternative but to accept the terms that were thrust upon them. Time to pay was the one concession they won. Campbell agreed that his army should at once retire to Rangoon upon payment of a quarter of the indemnity, or £250,000. Fifteen days were to be allowed for obtaining Bagyidaw's ratification, the delivery of the money and the return of all prisoners. British troops would evacuate Burma, apart from the ceded areas, upon payment of the next instalment, which was to be within one hundred days.

It was agreed, finally, that the king would sign a commercial treaty and should accept a British minister at Ava and send one himself to Calcutta, not to the court of St James, for which the Burmese argued forcefully, on the grounds that Calcutta was a mere dependency. Winning military domination first, the British thus extended the Empire by negotiation under the implied threat of further action.

The period of grace was to end on 18 January and for the next two weeks fraternisation between the two sides brought a little relief to the barren lives of the invaders, who discovered to their surprise that far from being savages, the Burmese were in some respects more civilised than they were.

Then came an anti-climax. It was seen that at night times especially the enemy worked hard at improving their defences, almost as if they knew that nothing conclusive would follow the agreement, except a renewal of war. On 17 January it appeared to Campbell that he had been tricked in the most barefaced way, for enemy envoys informed him that neither the ratification, nor the money or the prisoners had arrived from Ava. Instead, they offered to pay a lesser sum than the first instalment of £250,000, but only on condition that the British retired to Prome.

Campbell refused this out of hand, but he proposed that if the Burmese army retired within 36 hours from Minhla towards Ava, the British would follow, without starting hostilities again, and directly the treaty arms were complied with the march upon Ava would be reversed.

This very clever proposal having been promptly rejected, Campbell denounced the truce and let it be known that he would wage war again from midnight that day, 18 January 1826. He decided to make short work of the enemy this time. From dawn, every available gun, twenty-eight in all, hammered the enemy defences and afterwards the troops attacked from two sides.

The enemy seemed now to have no stomach at all for fighting. Perhaps the truth had leaked out – that Bagyidaw's treasury was now empty and he was finding it hard to raise the money to pay even this first instalment of the indemnity.[2] At all events, in a very short time the British stormed the stockade with only forty casualties, driving the enemy out with severe loss and seizing all their guns and stores.

Campbell felt that he had been fully justified in re-opening hostilities when it was reported to him that both the English and Burmese copies of the treaty were found in Prince Memiaboo's house, in the same state as when signed and sealed at the final meeting on 3 January. The sum of 40,000 rupees (about £4,000) in the prince's house was seized as prize money.

Campbell had ordered a messenger to hurry after the retreating Burmese with the unratified treaty and a letter to the Kee Wungyi saying that in the hurry of their departure they had forgotten a document which his Government might now find more useful and acceptable. The Wungyi politely returned his thanks for it, but added that in their hurry they had also left behind a large sum of money, which they were sure the British general only waited an opportunity of returning.[3]

Yet all the British present at the negotiations believed that the Burmese envoys were sincere in their wish to end the war there and then, by treaty. Perhaps they had overstepped their powers, or perhaps the king himself had second thoughts and had returned the documents unsigned. Later reports said Bagyidaw flew into a furious rage on hearing the British terms, wounded the messenger with a spear and sent down orders to fight another battle.

A week later, with his men rested and a few hundred cattle driven in from the countryside, Campbell resumed the march on Ava through the barren countryside of the oil wells. On 31 January, six liberated British prisoners walked into his camp bringing messages from the Kee Wungyi pleading for the best peace terms that Campbell would grant. Campbell merely varied the old terms slightly and agreed not to pass a certain town before twelve days, so as to allow time for the money to come down from Ava.

He then marched on with all speed and by 8 February was within a day's march of Pagan, where he learned for certain that despite their pleas, the Burmese were preparing still another stand. Having sent two brigades to gather forage he was down to a mere 1,300 fighting men, but these, he decided, would have to suffice. After a march through jungle, where Burmese troops harried his men with constant hit-and-run attacks, the column emerged into open country and found facing them a surprise Burmese force of some 20,000 men, deployed in a crescent formation with the flanks set forward in prickly jungle that ran on each side of the road. They were commanded by a new general, the Na-wing Phuring, the self-styled Prince of Darkness, who had forsaken the stockade system for fighting in the open field, in front of the shining white and gold Loganunda Pagoda.

Campbell at once instructed General Cotton to attack the left wing with HM's 38th and 41st, supported by the 43rd Madras Native Infantry and two guns, while he attacked the right with the 13th Light Infantry, HM's 89th, a small detachment of the Bodyguard and four guns. Campbell and his personal escort were surrounded all at once by a mass of enemy cavalry and in danger of being cut to pieces. The Bodyguard spurred their horses against the enemy, fell back until within range of the guns, then filed off so that these could check them until more troops came up and drove them from the field.

The attacks on the enemy flanks then drove them back to a field-work, whence the British dislodged them by the bayonet. They tried to rally inside the walls and about the pagodas of Pagan and for five hours fought a losing battle until this last hope of King Bagyidaw was finally routed. The 'Prince of Darkness' escaped into the jungle and thence to Ava to beg for another chance against the rebel foreigners. He was ordered from the king's presence, tortured and executed.

On 13 February two British prisoners, now freed, arrived at Campbell's HQ with the news that Bagyidaw had given in and accepted the terms, without bringing with them either the money or the ratified treaty, but asking on the king's behalf if the British would accept part of the indemnity now and the rest when it had retired to Prome. Campbell refused and again began the march to Ava. Bagyidaw gave as his reasons for this that he believed that having got the first £250,000 the British would then refuse to leave. The truth was that his privy council couldn't raise at once more than the fraction he offered, the equivalent of about £50,000, and finally the queen made a personal loan of £200,000 from her own resources.[4]

Through a rich and peaceful country with the river banks thickly studded with temples, monasteries, pagodas and villages the army continued to advance, reaching Yandabo, 45 miles from Ava, before meeting two of Bagyidaw's ministers of state bringing with them the money and the ratified treaty. It was finally signed by both sides once more on 24 February 1826, at Yandabo, the Burmese government agreeing at the same time to provide enough boats to transport most of the force back to Rangoon.

On 7 March, Sir Archibald Campbell and the first contingent of troops embarked in boats for Rangoon and, proceeding in a leisurely way, arrived there about two weeks later. The rest of the army followed in boats of various kinds and sizes and by the end of March the whole force had sailed for India, except for the detachment left to occupy Rangoon until payment of the second instalment of the indemnity. It was paid within the specified one hundred days, but six years passed before the balance was settled.

Thus ended the First Burmese War. Only the navy and fighting troops, British and Indian, officers and men, saved it from becoming a disaster on the scale of the First Afghan War, some fifteen years later. General Campbell made mistakes, inevitably, under the circumstances, for mismanagement by Lord Amherst, Governor-General, and General Paget, the C-in-C in India, faced him with an appalling problem in terms of transport, provisions and climate.

Had the king and his privy council continued their policy of laying waste the countryside and retreating north they would sooner or later have brought the British to their knees, starved of supplies, out of reach of naval help, because in the dry months of February, March and April the upper waters of the Irrawaddy subside into a stream that is barely navigable.

Disease and bad food nearly put Campbell's force out of action. Of the 3,500 British troops, exclusive of Sepoys and of officers, who originally landed in Rangoon, 150 only were killed owing to enemy action, compared with nearly 3,000 from disease and sickness. Of about 150 officers, 16 were killed in action and 45 died from disease. Of 1,004 British troops in Arakan, 595 died there, from cholera, malaria and dysentery, while of those who left not more than half were still alive after twelve months.[5] It was for the army beyond argument the most miserable, wretched and badly managed of all the wars to date that had made the British Empire. It cost 5 million pounds.

On the other hand, the British had won control of the Bay of Bengal from Cape Cormorin to Tenasserim and had, with this increase in territory, laid the foundation for a still bigger increase at the expense of Burma. For having regard to the pride and ambition on both sides another Anglo-Burmese war soon became simply a matter of time.

9

The Second War

King Bagyidaw hated the very thought of his defeat and of the treaty that the British had imposed upon him. But he did not learn any lessons from it, try to profit by it through learning the principles of western diplomacy, or even try to learn something of European military science. Instead, he brooded over his misfortunes, lost his cordial, joyous manner and grew sour and bitter. The country was impoverished after two years' war and the payment to the British of the huge indemnity; his treasury was almost bankrupt, while the loss of Arakan and Tenasserim, from which he and his family had derived much of their income, deprived his court of much of its former wealth and colour.

The commercial treaty signed on 23 November 1826 with Britain did very little to facilitate trade between the two countries. Rice the Burmese flatly refused to export because it was the people's staple food and at the time there was not a big enough surplus. Silver also they refused to export, because a huge amount having been handed over in part payment of the indemnity, they were anxious to conserve it for future payments, as well as to stop as much as possible the drain on the country's silver. Teak became the main trade commodity. By one means and another the Burmese also prevented a British resident being accredited to the court, fearing that he would

The Burma Wars

learn too much of their internal affairs. At the same time they flatly refused to send one to Calcutta because this was a mere dependency and not the court of St James. So from the first days of peace there was little to heal the wounds of war.

But in 1830, two years after the advent as Governor-General of Lord William Bentinck, a statesman of liberal outlook, whose understanding of the conquered nation led to less strained relations, Major Henry Burney became the first British Resident. A scholar and linguist, he studied Burmese history and won the court's regard, including even that of King Bagyidaw. Meantime, Bagyidaw's increasingly frequent fits of depression worsened until he became deranged and the queen, with her brother Menthagyee, took over direction of affairs of state. 'Their avaricious and grasping nature are involving the country in disaffection and ruin,' reported Dr Bayfield, a member of Burney's staff, perhaps a little oblivious of the overwhelming ruin to which the war and the indemnity had brought it.

In 1837, Prince Tharrawaddy, the king's brother, who had organised a large personal following of bandit chiefs, dacoits and disbanded soldiers, launched a determined rebellion against Bagyidaw and advanced upon the sacred royal palace-fortress. In no time at all the dispirited royal troops gave way and Tharrawaddy seized the throne. Burney let him know that the traditional massacre of members of the royal family capable of opposing him would be viewed by the British with marked disfavour, and thus was able to prevent it.

Tharrawaddy now grew to believe that Burney was a spy and relations between the two became strained, not least perhaps because the king's new ministers were mainly military commanders who wanted a last desperate war with the British, even though the odds were against them. 'Either the golden umbrella or the grave,' they declared.[1] Burney reported to Calcutta that Tharrawaddy was violent and warlike.

Perhaps the evidence for this was the king's attempt to engage European artillery experts, just as the Sikhs had done in the Punjab, to cast cannon of bigger calibre than those of the British and to instruct his gunners properly, for he believed that inferiority in this respect was the main cause of the Burmese

The Second War

defeat. Burney began to believe that Tharrawaddy would revoke the Yandabo Treaty and in 1837 he urged the Governor-General 'to declare hostilities against His Majesty and frighten him into reason.'[2]

Adoniram Judson, the American missionary whom the Burmese had imprisoned during the last war, seemingly unable to forget the misery of his confinement, went farther than this and urged the British to go to war because, surprisingly, it was 'the best, if not the only means of eventually introducing the humanising influences of the Christian religion'.[3]

But war did not come yet. Tharrawaddy knew for one thing that he could not rely upon the Mon people of Lower Burma, having been forced to crush a formidable rebellion there in 1838-40. He also knew how badly his own forces compared with the British. His failure to retrieve his kingdom's lost territory caused him, like his brother Bagyidaw, to suffer deep depression and after several attempts at suicide he died insane in 1846, a victim, like his brother, of mental instability brought about largely by the reversal of Burma's fortunes.

His eldest son, the Prince of Pagan, succeeded him. Pagan Min, as he was known, has been damned by historians as a thoroughly deplorable monarch. He began his reign in the traditional way by publicly murdering by strangulation or the mallet all his royal rivals, their wives and children, in accord with a bloody but oft-followed palace tradition. Yet for the first few years of his reign he tried hard to restore good administration. He suppressed banditry upon the rivers, brought back a semblance of peace and crushed a number of rebellions, trying at the same time to rescue his country from the disgrace of being a mere dependency of Calcutta by efforts to establish direct diplomatic relations with Queen Victoria. Failing in this, however, he grew disillusioned and cynical, preferring to spend his time at cock fights, bare-fist boxing matches and at drinking bouts. Inevitably, government deteriorated and corruption, from viceroys to the humblest provincial official, grew rampant.

Against this background of growing anarchy the second war between Britain and Burma now loomed. The Treaty of Yandabo guaranteed the security of British merchants and commerce. Merchants and traders at Rangoon were not to be harassed by undue exactions or to be oppressed in any way, but in the British view Burmese officials, in recent years especially, had gone out of their way to heap insults upon them and weigh them down with unjust exactions. Injured Burmese pride on the one hand and prickly British arrogance on the other hardly made for peace and harmony.

Lord Dalhousie, a Scottish nobleman, aged 35, and a determined imperialist, had, since becoming Governor-General in 1848, overthrown the Sikhs in the Punjab and made Britain master of India. An eager annexationist, ready at all times to extend India's frontiers, by 1851 he was free from other wars and ready if need be to put troops again into Burma, although he would have preferred not to.

There had been no British representative in Rangoon for ten years. Merchants were now complaining of unjust taxes, harbour dues and levies amounting to extortion. The climax came when two British sea captains were charged with murder and various other offences and although there was no trial they were imprisoned and heavily fined.

The two mariners appealed to the Government of India to demand compensation of £1,920 for reimbursement of the fines and for unlawful imprisonment. Lord Dalhousie cut the indemnity to be demanded from the Burmese down to £920, but said that British subjects had a right to be protected by their own government 'from injustice, oppression and extortion'.

Commodore Lambert, a short-tempered and impetuous naval commander, was then ordered to sail to Rangoon with a squadron of men-of-war, first ascertain that the two captains had given a true statement of what had taken place, then demand the reparation from the Burmese governor of Rangoon. 'It is to be distinctly understood,' Dalhousie said in his instructions, 'that no act of hostility is to be committed at present, though the reply of the Governor should be unfavourable, nor until definite instructions regarding such hostilities shall be given by the Government of India.'[4]

So Dalhousie already saw war likely over this trifling issue of £900 and a quarrel of two ships' captains. But a letter to the

The Second War

King of Burma was first to be delivered before any act of war, should the Governor of Rangoon refuse to comply with the British demands.

Lambert's ship dropped anchor off Rangoon on 27 November 1851 and a number of merchants crowded on board and bombarded Lambert with complaints, some justified, others mere impudence. Among examples of the latter was that of a Mr Crisp, who having heard of the chance of war between Burma and Britain had at once sold the Burmese a cargo of arms. He now complained that they had not paid him and asked the British Government to intervene on his behalf.[5]

From the moment he arrived in Rangoon, Lambert seems to have gone out of his way both to humiliate the Burmese and to create a situation where war was inevitable. First, disobeying his orders, he wrote demanding reparations before collecting the written evidence justifying it. Second, without waiting for an answer he wrote personally to the prime minister enclosing the Governor-General's letter to the king, which he had been instructed to send only when all else failed. In a letter to the governor of Rangoon, enclosing these two letters, he said that he expected that 'every dispatch will be used for forwarding the same, and I hold you responsible for an answer being delivered in these waters within five weeks from this day.'

He then sent his interpreter to Calcutta to explain his actions. Dalhousie's two colleagues on the Council of the East India Company would not accept the evidence he supplied to justify Lambert's disregard of his instructions. Dalhousie himself, however, supported Lambert's cutting short talks with the governor and sending the letter to the king at once. Meantime, Dalhousie warned Lambert that if the king failed to give a satisfactory answer, the British Government could not 'tamely submit ...' Reparations must be exacted, but without 'recourse to the terrible extremity of war, except in the last resort and after every other method has been tried without success.' He objected to bombarding Rangoon because it would be 'unjustifiable and cruel in the extreme, since the punishment would fall chiefly on the harmless population.' Equally, he objected to the armed invasion of Rangoon or Martaban because it would 'render inevitable the war which we desire in the first instance by less stringent measures to avert.' He therefore advised a blockade of Rangoon after first embarking British subjects there.[6]

But on 1 January 1852 the king answered in terms of seeming compliance. He declared that having regard to the friendship between the two countries 'we have recalled the Governor of Rangoon to the Golden Foot', adding that another suitable governor would be appointed while inquiries would be instituted with regard to merchants who had been unjustifiably ill-treated.

Honour appeared to have been satisfied. Dalhousie declared that this reparation ought to be accepted as fully satisfactory and advised that the inquiry should concern only the incidents of the ships' captains and no other matters. The shadow of war now seemed to be fading.

The king acted quickly. A new governor arrived on 4 January, but now Commodore Lambert undid all the good that had been done. Instead of going himself to meet the new governor, he sent an assistant interpreter named Edwards to request the removal of an embargo on communication between local residents ashore and Lambert's squadron. This the new governor immediately granted. With arrant discourtesy, Lambert then again disdained to meet the governor, but sent Captain Latter and Edwards, accompanied by two ships' officers, to his house to deliver a letter containing the demands for a settlement. Edwards went ahead and rode into the courtyard on horseback, defying the convention that even the most senior officials of any nationality should dismount. What occurred then is described by Captain Latter:

> At the foot of the outer steps one of the Governor's suite drew his dagger on him, threateningly asked him how he dared thus to approach the Governor's house. Mr Edwards replied that he had no intention of entering without the Governor's permission. On being called into the Governor's presence, he stated that his life had been threatened, and mentioned what had occurred. The Governor sent for the offender and punished him in the presence of Mr Edwards in the usual Burmese manner, namely by having him taken

The Second War

by the hair of the head, swung round three times, his face dashed to the ground, himself dragged out by the hair and pitched down the stairs.[7]

When this violent ritual had been completed, Edwards told the governor that a deputation of officers sent by Commodore Lambert would shortly arrive with a request for an interview. And now began the train of trivial circumstances that in Lambert's hands would be fashioned into war.

The governor, while ready to grant interviews informally to a junior official like Edwards, objected to having to disregard protocol to the point of granting the same favour to a body of senior officers, instead of a ceremonial reception, since he would lose face. He therefore told Edwards that he would accept the letter from him only. Edwards answered that this was impossible, since the deputation would be arriving at any moment, and he then left the governor's presence.

Shortly after, the deputation and Mr Kinkaed, an American missionary, rode together into the courtyard without dismounting. Having learnt their lesson the guards were this time more cautious, and merely asked them to wait because the governor was asleep. But the deputation apparently objected, left the courtyard and rode back to Lambert's ship, declaring that the governor had refused to see them.

Lambert, evidently a devout believer in gunboat diplomacy, decided to take the sternest possible action. Impatiently brushing aside the very shadow of protocol by failing to await a message from the governor, and disregarding the king entirely, he warned British residents ashore to be ready to leave Rangoon at once. Something like panic seems to have followed, because several hundred of them were rowed out to one or other of the British vessels anchored opposite Rangoon and that evening they sailed off down river.

Directly it was dark, in his heavy-handed way Lambert played what he must have felt was his trump card by illegally ordering the seizure of the king's yacht anchored nearby. He then issued a declaration of blockade of the Rangoon river and the Bassein and Salween rivers above Moulmein. And he capped these actions

The Burma Wars

by sending a letter to the king saying that all communication between British India and the Burmese Empire was suspended.

The next day, 7 January, at dawn, the squadron sailed down river with the King of Burma's ship in tow, and dropped anchor below the town of Dalla on the opposite shore. The governor of Dalla now interceded with Lambert, who said that out of his personal regard for him, he would reopen negotiations with his colleague, if that official would first come aboard his ship and 'express his regret for the insult he had offered to the British flag' by refusing to meet the deputation.

It was high-handed stuff indeed, but some time later the aged governor of Dalla hobbled back on board with a letter saying that the governor of Rangoon really was asleep, that he didn't want to see subordinate officers, and politely invited Lambert to visit him to settle all matters together, instead of leaving it to inferiors. Though he knew full well that this was the correct course, Lambert rejected the invitation, seemingly wishing to humble the Rangoon governor. And he sent a message saying that suitable measures would be taken unless the governor came on board his ship by noon next day.

Early in the morning of 8 January, the Dalla governor again came on board, this time to plead with Lambert to release the king's ship, because now being anchored in waters under his jurisdiction he would be held responsible, and punishment for its loss visited in part at least upon him. Lambert said no, and merely extended his ultimatum from noon till sunset. The day passed in waiting, then just before sunset Lambert received a message from the governor of Rangoon threatening to open fire upon him should he attempt to tow the king's ship out of the river. Lieutenant William Laurie, of the Madras Artillery, declared that the hot-tempered Lambert replied that 'if even a pistol were fired he would level the stockades with the ground.'

At dawn on 9 January 1852, Lambert ordered the squadron and the merchantmen to pass down the river. 'At length, the *Hermes* came in sight, rounding the point with the Burmese prize-vessel in tow,' reported Laurie.[8]

As she passed the stockade, guns in rapid succession were

opened on the vessels of war; at the same time, volleys of musketry were discharged upon them. The *Fox* immediately returned the enemy's fire by a terrific broadside; she likewise thundered forth against the war-boats which had ventured into the river.

The *Hermes* came up and poured forth her shot and shell into the line of stockade. The *Phlegethon* steamer, likewise, did vast destruction to the works. For nearly two hours were our vessels employed in spreading ruin and dismay around. During the conflict, a large gun-boat, having on board a gun of considerable calibre and upwards of sixty armed men, was sunk by a broadside, when nearly all on board perished. Altogether about 300 of the enemy were killed and about the same number wounded, in this first encounter with the Burmese.

And so began Commodore Lambert's war, a consequence of his arrogance and hot temper – 'the terrible extremity of war' which Dalhousie had expressly warned him to try to avoid. While the gun-smoke still swirled between the ships and the stockades Lambert sent a letter to Mr Hillady, secretary to the Government of India. 'It is with deep regret that I have had to commence hostilities with the Burmese nation, but I am confident that the Marquis of Dalhousie and the Government of India will see it was unavoidable, and necessary to vindicate the honour of the British flag,'[9] he wrote.

Having by seizure of the king's personal ship while the two nations were still at peace committed an act of piracy, Lambert had every reason to shout about the honour of the flag. And whatever happened, he was determined upon war. But on 11 January, despite the damage and loss of life done by the naval bombardment, the governor of Rangoon still looked to negotiations, rather than war. Four non-British foreign merchants in Rangoon, with the governor's approval, sent Lambert a petition stating that the governor agreed to pay the £900 demanded as compensation; to agree to a British Resident and to have a Residency house built, and to abide by the provisions of the Yandabo Treaty. The petitioners 'most humbly entreated' Lambert to have pity upon them, and to save them from ruin and destruction.

This petition, sent with the governor's approval, Lambert ignored. Yet, as Dalhousie stated in a minute to his colleagues on the Council on 22 January 1852, it left the door open for negotiations and the restoration of harmony between the two peoples. Dalhousie's criticism, expurgated in great part from the Government *Blue Book* published later to justify the war when an outcry followed in Parliament, declared that Lambert himself bore the entire responsibility for the succession of hostile acts which, unfortunately, both sides had undertaken. For Dalhousie believed that Lambert had no cause to seize the king's ship and that by doing so he made a move that inevitably caused the Burmese to react in a hostile way, as a result of which the two nations were now faced with the threat of war.

Dalhousie and his colleagues on his Council still seem to have wanted to avoid war at this time. Yet although they reprimanded Lambert for disobedience they did not have him removed to where he could do less harm. Lambert carried on blockading the Burmese coast. Meanwhile, on 7 February the king sent a letter to Dalhousie through Colonel Bogle, commissioner of Tenasserim, asking pointedly whether Lambert had been appointed to dispose of the issue of the ships' captains, or 'begin by an attack, which should have the effect of bringing on hostilities between the two countries'.[10] It was a chance for Dalhousie to repudiate Lambert's action, but he disregarded it.

On 2 February the governor of Rangoon wrote to Colonel Bogle saying that he awaited the arrival of an officer with whom the return of the king's ship could be arranged and to whom the payment of the £900 could be made. It disregarded Lambert's presence entirely and far from expressing regret for the alleged insult to the British flag, declared that the English officers had simply thrown all the blame on the other side so as to shield themselves.

The letter, Dalhousie declared, evaded making the required concessions. It was apparently at this time that he finally decided upon war. 'This letter leaves to the Government of India in my

The Second War

deliberate judgment ... no alternative but to exact reparation by force of arms.'[11] And on 13 February he repeated this in a letter to Lambert, for whom it must have been a triumphant occasion. Dalhousie added that a considerable force would sail from Bengal and Madras soon after 25 March.

Dalhousie knew well enough, however, how weak was the logical basis for war – simply the governor of Rangoon's very reasonable letter. He therefore sent the king an ultimatum, whose terms would be impossible for him to accept. After a preamble stating that it was still within the king's power to avert the disasters of war by full compliance, it demanded: (1) That the king himself, through his ministers, should apologise to him for the insult shown to the deputation of officers at the governor's residence on 6 January; (2) The king must pay at once an indemnity of ten lakhs (£100,000) for the British Government's expenses of preparation for war, for the loss of property which British subjects may have suffered in the burning of Rangoon by the acts of the governor, and in satisfaction of the claims of the two captains; (3) The king must accept and treat with due respect a British Representative at Rangoon; (4) Rangoon and Martaban must be ceded until the indemnity is paid.

The ultimatum was due to expire on 1 April 1852. Having no doubt that the king would find it impossible to comply Dalhousie went ahead with plans for the military expedition, appointing Lieutenant-General Henry Godwin, aged 69, who had served as a colonel in the First Burmese War, to command it. He instructed him to stay military operations only if the king agreed to the demands, or appeared ready to do so as soon as possible.

But King Pagan was by now convinced that the British had decided on war and that even if he did accede to the ultimatum's demands, worse demands would certainly follow. He knew without a shadow of doubt that his armies would be routed by the British, but believed it was better to fight and be conquered than suffer endless humiliation. Prince Mindon, his deeply religious brother, urged acceptance of the terms, to avoid bloodshed, but the king refused to answer the ultimatum[12] and

The Burma Wars

prepared for the war that would follow. 'Either the golden umbrella or the grave', became the cry once more.

Godwin's force was timed to reach Rangoon around the beginning of April, or about six weeks before the rains came. The hope, he noted in his journal, was that 'a powerful blow struck now may reduce the Burmese to reason' and so avoid a more extended war later in the year when the rains would be over.

The logic behind this was to a great extent based on the increased striking power of the British and what was assumed to be decreased Burmese military power. For about the last ten years the well-tried *Brown Bess* flintlock had been superseded in the British Army by the percussion-cap musket, which fired the charge by a flash through a hollow nipple. This cut out the time-wasting process of priming the pan with powder which was so often made useless by rain or damp, and also reduced the number of misfires in a thousand shots from 411 with the *Brown Bess* to as little as 4.5 with the percussion-cap. Accuracy had improved, as well as speed and reliability, with an average increase of 270 to 385 hits in 1,000 shots on a target. Artillery was more efficient and destructive, especially in the navy, whose guns could now shoot the heaviest shot and shell accurately between two and a half and three miles.

By 6 April 1852 both the Bengal and the Madras Infantry Brigades were gathered at the mouth of Rangoon river in transports escorted by a fleet of men-of-war commanded by Admiral Austen (Jane's brother). All of them were steam-driven, with auxiliary sail, and armed with 8-inch guns, 32-pounders and numerous smaller guns. The Bengal Brigade consisted of HM's 18th (later Royal Irish Regt) and 80th (later 2nd Btn South Staffordshires) and the 40th Bengal Native Infantry; the Madras Brigade, of HM's 51st, (later King's Own Yorkshire Light Infantry) and the 5th, 9th and 35th Madras Native Infantry, supported by two companies of Bengal Artillery, three of Madras Artillery and two companies of Madras Sappers and Miners, about 6,000 in all.

In accordance with his instructions, Godwin set about occupying Martaban first, just north of Moulmein, capital of the

The Second War

British occupied province of Tenasserim. He sailed there on 3 April and arriving before the strongly fortified town two days later, requested the warships to bombard it. It was a pattern for the rest of the war. In a short time the heavy shot and shell had shattered the defences. When the troops landed they found almost no resistance; those of the defenders who were not dead or wounded had run away into the jungle. By 8 April the force had returned to Rangoon with almost no casualties.

Here, on the glassy brown water, the heat hovered between 95 and 103 degrees Fahrenheit, knocking out officers and men one after the other with heatstroke. Cholera had started its deadly round and Godwin made haste. Five warships steamed up river on 11 April, Easter Sunday, and bombarded the stockades on each bank. 'The fire from the vessels, Queen's and Company's, was kept up with terrific effect against Dalla, on our left, and the Rangoon defences on our right,' noted Lieutenant Laurie, Madras Artillery, who was there.

At first, the enemy returned the fire with considerable dexterity and precision; but shortly after the *Fox* had come up and poured in her broadside, and the *Serpent* had moved on to destroy, by about eleven o'clock the firing on our right had almost ceased. However, the war-steamers kept on, thundering forth against the works on both sides of the river, utterly destroying the stockades on the shore at Rangoon, and cannonading Dalla with decided effect. The large stockade, south-west of the Shwedagon, was set on fire by a well-directed shell, which caused the explosion of a powder magazine; and then, all the work soon became filled with black smoke and vivid flame – up, up, right to the bright skies ascending, till the scene became one of extreme beauty and awful grandeur.... The stockade at Dalla having been silenced, a party of seamen and marines in four boats effected a landing and took the place by storm.

And so, Easter Sunday's operations were complete. 'The navy,' Laurie remarked, 'had acted as a pioneer of true civilisation.'

The Burma Wars

All was ready for the landing the next day, but it was not to be such a walkover as in 1824. The Burmese had built a new Rangoon about a mile inland behind the ruins of the former town. Approximately rectangular, it included the Shwedagon in the north-eastern corner and was entirely protected by a deep ditch, an abattis and a mud wall sixteen feet high and eight feet wide. Some 20,000 men manned the walls, in which were known to be placed about twenty guns, but it was well within the range of the fleet's heavy artillery.

Early on 12 April, the troops landed under a sustained fire from the warships, and amid the dumps of ammunition, beef rations, jars of arrack and scaling ladders all in a confused heap, formed two columns. Godwin moved off with the first column, intending to follow a roundabout route and attack from the east. With him in the advance were four Bengal artillery guns under Major Reid, covered by four companies of the 51st Light Infantry.

Godwin had not gone far, when they were fired on by enemy guns in the White House stockade, about a mile inland, to the east of the town defences. At the same time Burmese infantry attacked his left flank from a nearby jungle. They were driven off, and Major Reid fired at the stockade with his four guns at about 800 yards range. Soon, he turned to Godwin and said calmly: 'I am sorry to say, sir, that unless Major Oakes comes up we shall not be able to go on. I have but two rounds a gun left.'[13]

Burmese shot whistled close by and two gunners were killed. The situation was dangerous and unpleasant, but not critical, because four companies of the 51st could hold off any attack by enemy skirmishers.

At that moment Major Oakes led in two creaking and rattling 24-pound howitzers, drawn slowly by teams of panting seamen. Standing in the intensely hot sun, scarlet in the face in his thick blue uniform, he ordered his gunners to open up with spherical-case shot (shells) on the White House. Thirty minutes later he had fired his last round. He then collapsed unconscious with heatstroke and died soon after.

Godwin had meantime ordered the four companies of the 51st

The Second War

and the Madras Sappers to advance on the stockade and take it by storm, but the Burmese held them back by another flank attack. Having repulsed it, the storming party marched calmly forward and under heavy fire placed their ladders, forced an entry and took the place by storm, though with considerable loss. Meanwhile, though it was not yet mid-day, the terrific heat had killed another officer, Major Griffiths, knocked out three more and laid low numerous men.

It was foolhardy to continue; Godwin gave orders to set fire to the occupied stockade, rest in the shade for the rest of the day and camp where they were for the night on the open plain.

'The night of 12 April will long be remembered by many of the force,' noted Laurie.

> Towards the new town, and the great Shwedagon, fire continued to spread through the darkness – observing which formed amusement for the weary who could not sleep. It proceeded from the steamers and men-of-war pouring their destructive fire into the town. Huge hollow shot ... were continually projected, doing fearful execution. Sometimes, the effect from our camp, was terribly sublime.

Still not satisfied that the bombardment had flattened the defences enough to make an attack feasible without heavy losses, Godwin again rested his troops in the intense heat next day while the sailors laboured to drag up four eight-inch howitzers. In the dappled shade of the clumps of green bamboo, or the shadow of great trees, the troops stripped off their heavy red serge tunics and discussed yesterday's operations, cleaned their percussion muskets, polished and sharpened their bayonets, while the gunners cut and fixed fuses in the shells, so that all was ready for an all-out attack next day.

Reconnaissance parties had meanwhile reported that the Pagoda's eastern face where the defences were least strong offered the easiest entry. The route to it lay between alternate open plain, clumps of trees and thick shadowy jungle and here, when the troops moved forward at six o'clock on 14 April,

The Burma Wars

Burmese skirmishers fired volleys at the clustered red targets. The gunners fired a dozen rounds of grape-shot through the foliage and knocked them down, but when the troops emerged from the jungle they came within range of enemy jingals, which, firing from a small pagoda, killed several men until, at about ten o'clock, the howitzers came up and silenced them.

At 11.30 a.m. the storming party, four companies of the 80th, two of the 18th and two of the 40th Bengal Native Infantry, formed up on a small plain sheltered by a jungle-covered hill, ready for the attack. Shot from enemy guns whistled overhead, but soon the Burmese improved their elevation and men began to fall, the first being Dr Smith, Assistant-Surgeon. Burmese infantry had by now closed in near enough to hit the waiting masses of troops with accurate fire, but Godwin stubbornly waited for the heavy howitzers to finish their work until, says Laurie, Captain Latter, one of his aides, impatiently urged on him that they should attack forthwith, because, he said, for every ten men now being killed or wounded they might well lose only one with a storming party. Godwin, however, still preferred to wait and the troops went on bobbing their heads as the enemy shot whistled by.

Eventually, Latter asked if he might lead the storming party himself at once: 'With the greatest pleasure, my dear friend,' Godwin said coolly, to the surprise of all. The hill on which the great Pagoda stands was divided into three terraces, with four flights of steps, upon each of which enemy guns were mounted, and these were the storming party's target.

In column, led by Latter, the troops crossed the open valley leading to the ascent to the Pagoda, silent and steady under the heavy fire, till they reached the rising ground, when they ran forward and rushed with a great shout up the long flights of steps through the smoke from musketry and cannon. Having gained the upper terrace they spread out and soon drove all the enemy before them with the bayonet. The Burmese fled in all directions and, seeing the position taken so easily, the troops gave a loud cheer. More than 90 heavy guns, about 80 smaller ones and much ammunition were captured. In the three days' fighting, from 12 to 14 April, the British lost 132 wounded and

The Second War

17 killed, all ranks. Most of the Burmese defenders had deserted during the night.

The whole of Rangoon was in British hands. Two or three weeks of inactivity now followed, during which, in the intense heat, cholera again flared. Finally, having been reinforced with the 67th Bengal Native Infantry, Godwin embarked some 800 men in three warships and a naval brigade in a fourth, sailed down the Rangoon river and thence up the Negrais to attack Bassein on 19 May, which fell on the same day with a mere twenty-three casualties, all ranks.

So far so good, but the rainy season had begun, and despite these successes the Burmese had shown no inclination to ask for terms. The troops whiled away the intervening time as best they could, hunting for treasure in the temples and huge images. Laurie saw one soldier hacking away at a huge gilded image with a pick-axe on the Shwedagon's upper terrace. 'He is looking into the creature's heart and head for treasure – gold or small silver figures, or rubies.... This sacred spot is really one vast idol-shrine,' he noted.

At the end of May, hearing that the Peguese had risen in strength against their Burmese rulers, Godwin decided to send an expedition fifty-five miles north to take Pegu town. On 3 June, two companies of infantry, with sappers and miners, and a small party of marines and sailors, set forth under Major Cotton and Commander Tarleton. They stormed Pegu two days later, when the Burmese fled without firing more than a few shots. For political reasons it was garrisoned by indigenous troops, the Talaings, but after a few weeks the Burmese reappeared and drove them out, so the whole undertaking was a waste of time.

The war, which Dalhousie hoped would end quickly, had now gone on for three months and although the Burmese had been defeated at Martaban, Rangoon, Bassein and Pegu they showed no sign of accepting British terms. 'There is no symptom of submission,' Dalhousie[14] complained to a friend on 27 June.

I now give up all hope of it, except perhaps at a distant time, when our expenses will have risen to such a sum that the reimbursement we must demand will either be refused or can be met only by cession of territory – odious to them and undesired by us. Daily I am more mortified and disheartened by the political necessity I see before me...

Dalhousie therefore decided that his best course was to annex the entire province of Pegu, from Moulmein, in the south-east, to north of Prome, including of course, Rangoon and the entire Delta, so that henceforward Burma would have no outlet to the sea. And in London, Lord Aberdeen's Whig Government, which included Palmerston, readily accepted this.

Early in July, Commander Tarleton steamed up the Irrawaddy with a squadron of five warships, for some reason without any troops, to reconnoitre Prome's defences, and anchoring nearby on 9 July found no Burmese garrison holding it, but not having any troops himself, he could do nothing more than wreck the defences by gunfire and retire.

Dalhousie visited Rangoon on 27 July in the steam frigate *Feroze*, to study the situation at first hand. He decided that to carry out his plan of annexation reinforcements were needed to bring the total force up to two divisions totalling 20,000 men.[15] They arrived at Rangoon in September.

Colonel Reignolds's Brigade then sailed up river and dropped anchor before Prome on 9 October. The Burmese opened up with guns and muskets, but one or two heavy broadsides silenced them. Prome next day was found to have been deserted by the enemy, who had retired to a position ten miles to the east, so Godwin occupied the town and sent the flotilla back for another brigade of troops, returning to Rangoon himself some days later. Dalhousie began to criticise Godwin's leisurely way of fighting the campaign. He even thought of sacking him, but concluded, in a letter to a friend: 'He is a gallant old soldier and I am reluctant to do him a harm.'

Pegu had to be retaken, and Godwin himself led the force of about 1,000 men which landed in thick mist below the town on 21 November. It fell the next day, after an exhausting jungle march round to the town's eastern face and a short sharp fight in

The Second War

the jungle, but thereafter the Burmese carried out jungle guerilla operations, counter-attacking Pegu, cutting off British supplies, attacking their outposts, which prolonged operations there until mid-December.

A few days later, on 20 December, on behalf of Dalhousie, Captain Phayre, who was to be the commissioner of Pegu, announced the annexation of the entire province to the British. The document, which threatened the 'total subversion of the Burman State and the ruin and exile of the King and his race', if the annexation was not accepted quietly, ordered also that all Burmese troops were to be driven out of the province; and for this purpose General Steel set out from Martaban, in the south, on 14 January 1853, with 4,000 men and supporting artillery, to march to the northern boundary.

He took with him one month's supplies borne on the backs of 120 elephants and in 300 bullock carts, an extremely vulnerable supply line if the enemy was enterprising enough. But his march was practically unopposed, so that he arrived in Toungoo, on the province's northern border, almost without bloodshed, on 22 February, after a march of 240 miles through unexplored tropical forest.

British intelligence agencies at this time in Arakan and elsewhere had learned of conspiracies to dethrone Pagan Min and replace him by his brother Mindon Min, who was opposed to continuing the war. But this could not be counted on, and since the Burmese had not yet asked for negotiations, Dalhousie had been forced to accept the fact that he might yet have to march upon Ava to bring this costly war to an end.

Transport animals to pull the heavy guns and carry supplies were vital for such an operation. The army in Arakan had for this purpose assembled three hundred fully grown elephants, which by now were treading the forests and climbing the mountains of the Arakan Yoma range, on the hazardous route to Prome. Such a vast undertaking could hardly be kept secret, and the Burmese built a stockade near the start of the Aeng Pass to try to overcome the escort and seize the elephants. Scouts riding ahead of the great column winding its way up the mountains discovered the stockade in time. A force of Arakanese troops led by British officers seized the stockade in a surprise attack on the night of 6 January 1853, killed numbers of Burmese troops and scattered the rest. Soon the elephants entered the Irrawaddy valley via a pass about 100 miles south of Aeng and began to lumber into Prome early in March.

But, greatly to Dalhousie's relief, these costly preparations now became superfluous. On 18 February King Pagan was deposed and one of Mindon's first steps as successor was to send two Catholic priests as envoys to the British on a peace mission. Captain Phayre met them on 31 March at Meaday, fifty miles north of Prome, with a ready-made treaty, which included for cession to the British hundreds of square miles of valuable teak forests in the area between Prome and a track north of Meaday. It far exceeded the boundary of Pegu, defined in Dalhousie's proclamation of 20 December 1852. The Burmese objected strongly, and the issue was referred back to Dalhousie, who answered with a memorandum stating bluntly that 'the frontier of the British territory is fixed at six miles north of Meeaday.'[15] The Burmese were warned to respect this frontier and to remember that although the British wanted peace they were fully prepared for war, which could only mean the end of the Burmese state.

King Mindon had no alternative but to accept this *fait accompli*, but he refused to sign a treaty which embodied it. Dalhousie was a little cynical. 'Our real treaty is our military power, and I will take care that it is maintained,' he declared in a private letter to a friend.[17] Captain Phayre delivered the memorandum to the Burmese envoys on 10 May 1853 and broke off negotiations with them.

A cease-fire was finally declared on 30 June 1815, and thus the Second Anglo-Burmese War ended, having cost British and Indian taxpayers £1 million. There was little enthusiasm for it in England and the newspapers, including *The Times*, agreed that it was 'an inglorious war'. For there were feelings abroad then that to ruin and crush a small Oriental nation hardly added to the lustre of the British Empire. Informed men and women were somewhat ashamed to have to admit that a people entirely lacking in industrial techniques were being thrown

The 'Signal Pagoda', Rangoon, so called because it was used for signalling.
The National Army Museum

A photograph (taken by John MacCosh) of Commander Tarleton, R.N., who, with a squadron of five warships, destroyed the defences of Prome on the Irrawaddy in July 1852.
The National Army Museum

An early photograph, taken by John MacCosh, of Lieutenant-General Sir Henry Godwin who commanded British troops in the Second Burmese War.
The National Army Museum

Commodore Lambert, R.N., who bore the main responsibility for the Second Burmese War. He was described as 'combustible'. (Photograph by J. MacCosh)
The National Army Museum

A Burmese woman wearing a gold necklace, in an 1852 photograph taken by John MacCosh.
The National Army Museum

A Burmese peasant girl, photographed in 1852 by John MacCosh.
The National Army Museum

A Burmese boy in an 1852 photograph taken by John MacCosh.
The National Army Museum

An old ship gun, captured in Rangoon, 1852. The man on the left is probably John MacCosh, the photographer, timing an exposure.
The National Army Museum

Primitive weapons handicapped the Burmese fighting forces. Shown here is a war-axe, with a spare blade carried in the wooden sheath.
The Victoria and Albert Museum

The Second War

against the most powerful weapons which the manufacturing industry of England could put into the field.

Yet from the military standpoint Godwin's task was no easy one. The Burmese dacoits were, of course, a jungle guerilla force, so, like the Americans in Vietnam, he was faced with intimidated villagers on all sides as likely to betray him as tell him the truth. Sickness, in the form of malaria, dysentery and cholera also killed hundreds of his men. And he too seems to have been affected by his personal feelings about the rightness of the war to the extent that he hesitated about pursuing it with the maximum vigour.

Dalhousie believed the assurances he had received from missionaries and merchants that the Karens and the Mon people of Pegu would welcome British instead of Burmese rule, but instead, when the annexation became known both peoples revolted, while Burmese officials set up jungle resistance groups. One of these, Myat-Htoon, commissioner of the Danchen district, dominated an area north of Danubyu with his headquarters in a town or stronghold of 20,000 people, held by an armed force of 7,000 men. The first British attempt to overthrow him, when a force of about 600 men with guns marched against his stronghold, was ambushed and thrown back in February 1853 with more than eighty killed and wounded.

Brigadier-General Cheape with a force of 1,100 with two guns, including a 24-pounder howitzer and a few rocket tubes, was then given the task. It took him twenty-four days of hard jungle fighting, with the temperature around 95 degrees, before the task was completed, Myat-Htoon's force scattered and his power broken. The British lost 130 killed or wounded, among whom was Ensign Garnet Wolsely, later Lord Wolsely, whose thigh was ripped by an enemy shot, so that for ever after he walked with a limp. Cholera killed more than a hundred, all ranks.

But the defeat of Myat-Htoon did not end guerilla opposition to British rule, even though officially hostilities ended on 30 June 1853, with the Burmese ceding Pegu Province. Other chiefs came forward to replace him and terrorise people who had accepted alien rule. So difficult did the situation become that in September 1853 Phayre sought and received from Dalhousie the power of summary trial with the death sentence for anyone found carrying arms illegally, and not for another four years was political opposition to alien rule curbed, while dacoity and general lawlessness, as a form of protest, continued until beyond 1860. Thereafter, however, while the Burmese social fabric crumbled in British Burma, economically the region prospered.

Largely, the ending of the sumptuary laws relating to social status, the disappearance of the feudal *myothugyi* or hereditary township chief and his influence; the emergence of a money economy with wage labour and individualism under British rule, and the weakening of religious sanctions, robbed Burmese social structure of its former vitality. At the same time, from 1862 to 1883, British Burma's population rose by fifty per cent (2·5 million to 3·7 million), its trade increased five-fold and its revenues trebled. This very prosperity was soon to lead to cries for the annexation of independent Upper Burma in England and among the English merchant community in Rangoon.

10
The Third War and Annexation

Prince Thibaw had succeeded to the Burmese throne in 1878, upon the death of King Mindon in September of that year. The Kinwun Mingyi, or chief minister, and Mindon's chief queen, Sinpyumashin, had engineered his succession and his marriage to her daughter, Supayalat, because Thibaw lacked any personal political following and was in any case pliable. Evidently, the chief minister believed, wrongly as it turned out, the council of ministers would in these circumstances be able to rule without hindrance and carry out a programme of reform. But the two women, Queen Supayalat and her mother, aided by Taingda, a high functionary who was chief of the all-important Palace Guard, quickly seized the reins of power.

Almost at once the queen showed her true character by instigating the arrest of numerous royal relatives who could have challenged her and her husband's supremacy. Then came the blood-bath. Nearly a hundred of them, including eight princes, the king's step-brothers, were publicly executed by strangulation or mallet-blows upon the head, during a dazzling festival of music and dancing. British protests stayed some of these murders, which, in any case, the council of ministers, or *Hlutdaw*, had not authorised, but the Kinwun Mingyi explained blandly that there was a traditional basis for them, as a means of avoiding civil strife after the succession of a new king.

It gave the British in Rangoon their first solid grounds for intervention and annexation, but war in Afghanistan at the time ruled out military adventures in Upper Burma. Meanwhile, under Thibaw's ineffectual rule, corruption and banditry flourished wholesale, with rebels even controlling the town of Sagaing, almost facing the new royal capital of Mandalay across the Irrawaddy. News from Mandalay of public executions of numbers of known followers of two exiled princely contenders for the throne again gave rise to hopeful cries for annexation among British merchants in Rangoon.

In August 1885, blew up the incident that was the apparent cause of the Third Anglo-Burmese War, of the annexation of the remainder of the country and of the end of the monarchy. This was the ruinous fine ordered in Mandalay by the council of ministers of 23 lakhs of rupees (£2·3 million) on the Bombay-Burma Trading Corporation for allegedly having exported more teak logs than they had actually paid for. Obviously a commercial dispute subject to arbitration or negotiation, it was not a cause for war. Anglo-French rivalry in South-East Asia was the real trouble, but the affair of the teak logs, deeply involved as it was with powerful commercial interests, was likely to evoke a more bellicose response in the public mind than fears that French domination of Indo-China might succeed in spreading through Laos to unstable and chaotic Upper Burma, and even challenge the British in Lower Burma.

These fears took a turn for the worse, when French encouragement led to Thibaw's government sending a mission of six high officials to Paris in 1883 to arrange a treaty, on the face of it a commercial one, but believed by the British, despite French assurances to the contrary, to involve the supply of arms, especially French artillery. The Franco-Burmese Treaty was finally signed in 1885 and the mission, turning its back on England, then caused more British suspicion by meeting the Italian Government in Rome before going home.[1]

British fears were, of course, well-founded, for the Burmese, having lost much of their territory to them already, and knowing

The Third War and Annexation

the commercial pressures for annexation of the remainder, were trying with Oriental astuteness to use Britain's main rival in imperialism, France, to extricate themselves. But at this time, 1880-85, Gladstone's anti-imperialist government ruled in London, firmly opposed to solving the difficulty by war and annexation.

But briefly, from June to December 1885, Lord Salisbury's Tory government came to power. It coincided with reports that the French had negotiated the construction of a railway from Mandalay to Toungoo, which would link up with the British line from Rangoon, thus forestalling them in Upper Burma. In addition, the French had apparently arranged the establishment of a Burmese state bank, with a capital of £2·5 million, to issue currency. The necessary French loans were to be repaid from royalties from Burmese oil and river customs dues.[2]

This and other rumours of French concessions prompted Lord Dufferin, the then viceroy of India, to warn London of what he believed should be done to counteract French advances. 'We are unanimously of the opinion that the establishment by France of dominant or exclusive influence in Upper Burmah would involve such serious consequences to our own Burmese possessions and to India that it should be prevented even at the risk of hostilities with Mandalay,' he said in a telegram on 2 August 1885.

... Assuming that an agreement is contemplated by means of which the French would dominate trade and the chief sources of revenue in Ava, we think that immediate action should be taken to arrest the scheme.

We would propose on our side to address the Burmese Government in the terms proposed by Bernard, and to insist on reception and proper treatment of a British Resident, to whose advice in all matters of foreign policy we should require Burmese Government to submit. If those terms were refused, we should be prepared for measures of coercion ...

At the same time, we should consider it a misfortune on many accounts to be forced to adopt coercive measures

The Burma Wars

of this description. The time is most inopportune; we are opposed on principle to annexationist policy, and the acquisition of Upper Burmah would entail upon us considerable responsibilities.[3]

At this clear warning Lord Salisbury saw the French Ambassador, who, however, declared that he knew nothing of it, but would write to M. de Freycinet, the prime minister, about it. In September the Ambassador told Salisbury that the French Government also knew nothing about such agreements, but added that his government believed it would be wise, in view of the position occupied in the East by France, to open negotiations with Britain for a division of influence in the Indo-China peninsula, which, of course, meant Burma.

It was an ominous suggestion, in view of everything. Lord Randolph Churchill, Secretary of State for India, had not the slightest intention of dividing Burma with France. He knew now well enough that French policy was to secure the political ascendancy of France in Upper Burma to the disadvantage of England.

Commercial interests in Rangoon now intensified their campaign for annexation and thus the dispute over the teak logs with Mandalay in August intensified. Lord Dufferin on 16 October proposed to Lord Salisbury's government the sending of an ultimatum to Mandalay. The government gave consent on 17 October and on the 22nd a British ultimatum gave Mandalay until 10 November, less than twenty days, to accept an envoy with free access to the king, as well as his own warship and guard of 1,000, to accept British control of its foreign relations, to agree to arbitrate the Bombay-Burma fine and to grant proper facilities for British trade with China via Bhamo. Since the Burmese Government was likely to reject the ultimatum, three brigades of troops sailed at once for Rangoon under Major-General Prendergast ready for an immediate advance on Mandalay. Meantime, before the decision was known, both the London and the Glasgow Chambers of Commerce were petitioning the government for the 'immediate annexation of Native Burma, or the establishment of an efficient protectorate over it'.

The Third War and Annexation

In Mandalay, Queen Supayalat, King Thibaw and the Taingda decided that the ultimatum's terms were too humiliating to accept. Only the disgraced chief minister, the Kinwun Mingyi, summoned to the Hall of Audience, advised a conciliatory reply immediately in the hope that meantime international public opinion would make the British moderate their demands, but Queen Supayalat and the Taingda angrily dismissed him.

On 5 November the king informed the Governor-General that the fine was lawfully imposed and therefore not subject to negotiation, but the Corporation could petition about it. He agreed to accept a British Agent as he had before, but said he would refer to France, Germany and Italy the demand for control of Burma's foreign relations, since these countries were friends of both states.[4]

Queen Supayalat and the king knew well enough that their answer meant war, but blithely they had deceived themselves in the traditional manner about their military power. 'Those heretics the English *kalas* barbarians, having most harshly made demands calculated to bring about the impairment and destruction of our religion, the violation of our national traditions and customs, and the degradation of our race, are making a show and preparation as if to wage war with our State,' Thibaw declared in a country-wide proclamation on 7 November 1885.

> They have been replied to in conformity with the usages of great nations, and in words which are just and regular. If, notwithstanding, these heretic *kalas* should come and in any way attempt to molest or disturb the State, His Majesty ... will himself march forth with his elephants, captains and lieutenants, with large forces of infantry, artillery, elephanterie and cavalry, by land and by water, and with the might of his army will efface these heretic *kalas* and conquer and annex their country.[5]

In almost the same way King Bagyidaw had spoken when the British landed in Rangoon sixty-two years earlier. If the people no longer did, the king and queen still believed in the myth of their personal invincibility.

155

The Burma Wars

Directly the reply was known in London, on 11 November, Lord Randolph Churchill telegraphed to the Viceroy: 'Please instruct General Prendergast to advance at once.'

Major-General Sir Harry Prendergast, VC, CB, of the Madras Engineers, a veteran of the Mutiny, had assembled at Rangoon some 10,000 men consisting of three infantry brigades, British and Sepoy, with sixty-seven guns, supported by floating batteries of heavy modern artillery (70-pounders and howitzers), a naval brigade 600 strong and a body of volunteer cavalry.[6] A flotilla of armed naval steamships towed the troops up river in river steamers, barges and lighters equipped with awnings and adequate living quarters. Plumes of dark smoke marked its progress up the wide expanse of the great Irrawaddy on this expedition which was to be so fateful for the Burmese kingdom.

On 15 November the flotilla crossed the frontier into independent Burma and all that day steamed up river against the torrent. The first Burmese reaction occurred on the 16th, when Burmese artillery opened up from stockades on each side of the river. The heavy 70-pounders, known as 'Mother Carey's chickens', because Colonel Carey commanded them, fired a few rounds in reply, then the infantry landed and quickly carried both stockades.

Minhla now lay ahead, a town British intelligence knew to have been strongly fortified for Thibaw by two Italian experts, Majors Molinari and Comotto. Opposite, on the left bank, up on a hill, lay the fort of Gweg-Yaung Kamyo, also strengthened by the Italians and furnished with guns that commanded the river. Fortunately, there was reason to believe that the guns were antiquated and served by relatively untrained gunners.

Prendergast decided that his force was strong enough to attack both forts at once and early on 17 November he landed several battalions, British and Indian, two or three miles below them. Dense jungle separated the troops from their objectives and through its steamy heat they stumbled and cursed their way forward. Meanwhile, directly the flotilla rounded a bend in the river both forts opened up on it with gunfire. 'Mother Carey's chickens' began thumping away in reply and destroyed them

The Third War and Annexation

with accurate hits. When the infantry stormed the Gweg-Yaung Kamyo fort they encountered almost no resistance, for the violent bombardment had so demoralised those of the defenders who were not killed or wounded that nearly all of them fled.

Not so simple was the attack on Minhla itself. In the dense jungle the troops sometimes lost contact both with their officers and each other, until they were hit by sudden volleys from hidden enemy stockades. But the British were harder targets than in the former campaigns, now that khaki, which merged into the variegated yellow, green and brown of the jungle, had replaced the old scarlet tunics, so bright in the marksman's eye. The relatively light, easily drawn mountain guns quickly came up and expelled the enemy from their stockades, but they still fought stubbornly for every yard of territory, all the way to Minhla. Flames leapt skyward there, where shell fire from the flotilla had set it ablaze. Here too the Burmese bravely held their ground, until the British took the fort and town by storm, driving out the remnants of the enemy into a hail of fire from the flotilla.

In the ruins of the two forts Prendergast left garrisons and on 19 November sailed on up river. At Magwe a pleasant surprise awaited him. A boat bearing a flag of truce was rowed out into the river. It held two very downcast Europeans, the two Italian fortifications experts, who had decided that their future was more secure with the British than with King Thibaw, who had cruel ways of dealing with those who had displeased him. Farther up river at Nyaungu, enemy artillery on a cliff top began a cannonade, but it was child's play for the howitzers to silence them. Troops then landed and heaved the enemy guns down over the cliff top into the river.

Meanwhile, in Mandalay, it was learned later, the king and queen had received a message from their Commander-in-Chief, reporting a great victory over the British, who, he said, had been routed and driven back towards Rangoon. Supayalat was triumphant. She ordered a magnificent victory celebration. Music echoed beneath the vermilion and gold roofs of the palace, dancing girls performed their bizarre choreography in naked

The Burma Wars

joy. Thibaw drank, confident that the wild foreigners were actually routed, and Supayalat looked on with profound satisfaction.

Although in the capital there were already rumours that the British were steadily advancing and had passed Pagan on their way to Mandalay the Golden, nobody dared to tell the king and queen.

Through the steamy haze that rose from the river, the flotilla had sighted the large town of Myingyau at noon on 24 November. Here, it was believed the rest of the Burmese army awaited them, under the command of the Commander-in-Chief, and through their telescopes the British saw the golden umbrellas of the enemy chiefs as they inspected the troops assembled on the defences and stockades. Another deadly bombardment began from a distance beyond the range of the enemy artillery. When the smoke cleared, the British saw through binoculars and telescopes that the defenders had melted away. Prendergast landed his troops and they found the trenches and field works empty even of dead and wounded, hurriedly removed by the terrified enemy.

Barely ten days after the war had started, it was the end of the Burmese army, and of the fighting. Prendergast cannot have got much soldierly satisfaction from it and the troops certainly felt that they had been cheated of some good fighting. They were said to be morose and irritable for weeks afterwards. Prendergast had a proclamation read the next day in Myingyau promising due respect for religion, customs and private rights and assuring all that they could go about their callings provided they did not oppose the passage of the troops. Officials were called upon to help in preserving public order.

In Mandalay the thunder of the guns had at last revealed the bitter truth to the king and queen. In desperation Thibaw recalled the disgraced chief minister Kinwun Mingyi, who told him it was too late for negotiation and advised him to concede everything the British demanded. On 27 November, when the flotilla was within sight of Ava, Prendergast received a message from the king agreeing to surrender himself and his army. When Prendergast landed his troops at Ava the Burmese army had

The Third War and Annexation

melted away with its arms into the forest. Prendergast destroyed the artillery, resumed his advance up river and anchored off Mandalay on 28 November. Troops landed and with bands playing marched up to the royal capital in separate columns which entered the city through each of its different gates.

Mounted on an elephant, at one of the palace gates, Kinwun Mingyi met Colonel Sladen, the political representative, a former Agent who spoke Burmese, and told him that King Thibaw would see him at once. At the audience, which Supayalat also attended, Sladen said he would permit them to remain in the palace that night, but they must be prepared to leave Mandalay next day, for ever.

Women attendants of the queen were to be allowed that night to come and go through the palace gates. It was the signal for mass looting. Not only the royal serving women, but scores of women from Mandalay streamed into the palace and while the king and queen were under guard in their apartments took part in an orgy of looting the treasures of centuries, gold and silver, rubies and sapphires, coinage and sacred objects. At daylight, when this was revealed, a detachment of the Hampshires stopped all Burmese from entering.

When finally they were ready, Thibaw and Supayalat emerged through the gates of the royal palace in a simple bullock cart with a covered-in cab to protect them from the sun. Escorted by British troops they left the lacquered spires and pagodas of Mandalay the Golden for ever. Supayalat's poise never once deserted her. During the drive to the river she ordered the Burmese driver to stop, then leaning from the window of the coach she beckoned smilingly to a British soldier to give her a light for her cheroot.[7]

They went on board the steamship *Thooreah*, which at once cast off and sailed down river, escorted by warships. From Rangoon the couple sailed to India and were exiled to Ratnagiri fort, near Bombay. Thirty years later in 1916 Thibaw died and with him, for ever, the Burmese monarchy. After his death the Indian Government permitted Supayalat to return to Burma, where for some years she lived in a modest bungalow in Rangoon.

The Burma Wars

The old order faded like a dream after their departure and the abolition of the monarchy, upon which it was founded. The British had little respect for their surroundings. The magnificent Hall of Audience became a garrison church and upon the Lion Throne an altar was set up. An officers' club was opened amid the royal palace's gilded teak columns. The dancing girls and the strange music vanished.

How did the Burmese leaders and people react to this upheaval of their age-old traditions, customs and beliefs? Lawlessness on a country-wide scale was the first outcome. Disbanded soldiers without food or money formed wandering bands called dacoits and foraged the countryside. Village communities followed, for everyone felt acutely the lack of authority in the country caused by the end of the monarchy, especially in its role of Buddhism's patron and chief; and by the collapse of the traditional administrative system.

Soon this general lawlessness changed character into a widespread anti-British political movement, caused to a great extent by the severe penalties imposed by the army for the illegal possession of arms. Dacoits formed larger units for the express purpose of attacking the military outposts the British had established to impose order. In this way guerilla warfare against the British grew and expanded. General Prendergast ordered harsh punitive measures in return, including the shooting of anyone having arms, the burning of villages where resistance was met with and the flogging of those believed to be taking part in resistance.

The British proclamation on 1 January 1886 that Burma would henceforward become a province of British India only worsened the situation. Military outposts were increased from ten to twenty-five with patrolling between them by strong forces, whose task was to seek out and destroy the dacoit formations. At first little progress was made and by June 1886 a nation-wide rebellion had developed throughout Lower as well as Upper Burma, remarkable for the participation even of the yellow-robed monks. The Commander-in-Chief came over from India and ordered substantial reinforcements, the establishment of a Burmese field force and a more aggressive campaign to crush

The Third War and Annexation

the rebellion. But it took four years of hard campaigning and summary executions without proper trial before the Burmese gave up the unequal struggle in 1890.

Bitterness thereafter died, for the Burmese acknowledged that the new British officials ruled with justice and fairness in their efforts to bring order and prosperity to the country. Burmese customs did not completely decay, the national dress was not supplanted by European clothing, Buddhism remained the national religion, racial or social barriers did not arise to mar relationships between rulers and ruled, and a higher standard of living generally prevailed. The thirty years from 1890 meant growth and prosperity to Burma after the upheavals and insecurity of the past. Not until 1920 did the flames of nationalism begin to burn again, but that is another story.

CHAPTER 1
1. *A Prisoner in Ava*, H. Gouger (London 1830) p. 106
2. *The Stricken Peacock*, Maung Htin Aung, p. 30, The Hague, 1965
3. *Bengal Secret and Political Consultations*, vol. 91, 29 April 1802, No. 20
4. Op. cit. 29-April-1802, No. 23
5. Op. cit., vol. 96, 2 Sept. 1802, No. 2
6. Op. cit., vol. 135, 17 May 1804, No. 160a.
7. *Ibid*
8. Op. cit. quoted in *The Mauling of Burma*, p. 54, D. Woodman
9. *Documents Illustrative of the Burmese War*, compiled by H. Wilson, Calcutta, 1827, document 4
10. Op. cit., document 5
11. Op cit., document 6
12. Op. cit., document 7

CHAPTER 2
1. *A Description of the Burmese Empire*, Father San Germano, Constable, 1883, p. 80
2. *An Account of the Burman Empire*, Henry Ball, Calcutta, 1852.
3. *A History of Modern Burma*, John F. Cady, Cornell University Press, 1958, pp. 59-60

4. *An Embassy to the Court of Ava*, London, 1800, pp. 122-123
5. *Burma Past and Present*, A. Fytche, p. 80, London, 1878
6. Wilson, op. cit., document 23
7. *A Narrative of the First Burmese War*, G. W. De Rhé-Philipe, p. 35, Calcutta, 1895
8. Burmese Expeditionary Force:
Bengal Division: HM's 13th (became Somerset Light Infantry), HM's 38th (became S. Staffordshire Regt.), 40th Bengal Native Infantry, European Artillery
Madras Troops: HM's 41st (became Welsh Regt.), 102nd Regt. (Madras European Regt.), 1st Btn. Pioneers, 3rd Madras Native Infantry, 7th Madras Infantry, 8th, 9th, 10th, 17th and 22nd Madras Native Infantry, Madras Foot Artillery, HM's 89th (became 2nd Btn. Royal Irish Fusiliers), some of whom arrived in June and others in December 1824, Bombay Foot Artillery
9. Marshall, op. cit., pp. 4-5

CHAPTER 3
1. *Reminiscences of the Burmese War*, F. B. Doveton, p. 18
2. *The Naval Operations in Ava*, by John Marshal, p. 6
3. Doveton, op. cit., p. 20
4. *Narrative of the Burmese War*, Major Snodgrass, p. 8

CHAPTER 4
1. Document 33, *Documents Illustrative of the Burmese War*
2. Document 36, op. cit.
3. *Bengal Secret and Political Consultations*, 5 May 1826, No. 10
4. Desai, W. S., 'Events at the Court and Capital of Ava During the 1st Anglo-Burmese War', J.B.R.S., Vol. XXVII
5. Gouger, op. cit., p. 128
6. Crawfurd, *Embassy to Ava*, vol. II, Appendix

CHAPTER 5
1. Snodgrass, op. cit., p. 37
2. Ibid.
3. Document 57, Wilson, op. cit.

Notes

4. Doveton, op. cit., p. 70
5. Lieutenant John Marshall, *Naval Operations in Ava*, London, 1830, p. 16
6. Crawford, *Embassy to Ava*, vol. II, Appendix
7. Snodgrass, op. cit., Appendix I, p. 302
8. Snodgrass, op. cit., p. 302

CHAPTER 6
1. *Bengal Secret and Political Consultations*, 5 May 1826, No. 10
2. J. Marshal, op. cit., p. 56
3. *Bengal Secret and Political Consultations*, op. cit.

CHAPTER 7
1. Morrison's force: artillery; HM's 44th, 54th, 42nd, 2nd Battalion Light Infantry; 10th, 16th M.N.I.; 26th, 49th, 62nd, 7th, 14th, 39th, 44th, 45th, 52nd Bengal Native Infantry: Pioneers; 2nd Local Horse. (The 44th became Essex Regt.; 54th 2nd Btn. Dorsets; 42nd, the Black Watch
2. *Journal of the Burmese Research Society*, XXIX, II, 1939, p. 177
3. Op. cit., p. 157
4. Wayland, op. cit., pp. 281-2
5. Crawfurd, vol. II, op. cit., p. 128

CHAPTER 8
1. Snodgrass, op. cit., p. 224
2. Snodgrass, op. cit., pp. 263-5
3. Snodgrass, op. cit., p. 273
4. *Journal of the Burmese Research Society*, XXIV, Part III, p. 149
6. Wilson, op. cit., p. 288

CHAPTER 9
1. Maung Htin Aung, *The Stricken Peacock*, p. 38
2. *Bengal Secret and Political Consultations*, No. 35, Burnley's Letter, July 1837
3. *India Secret Proceedings*, vol. 8, Benson's Letter, July 1838

4. *Blue Book: Papers Relating to Hostilities with Burma*: Cmd. 1490, p. 14
5. Dorothy Woodman, *The Making of Burma*, p. 125
6. Cmd. 1490, pp. 31-32
7. Cmd. 1490, p. 44
8. W. F. B. Laurie, *The Second Burmese War*, p. 30
9. Cmd. 1490, p. 42
10. Cmd. 1490, p. 70
11. Op. cit., p. 64
12. *The Stricken Peacock*, p. 50
13. Laurie, op. cit., p. 71
14. Dalhousie, *Private Letters*, pp. 207-8
15. Bengal Division, Brigadier-General Sir John Cheape. *1st Brigade*, Col. Reignolds; HM's 18th (Royal Irish Regt.), 40th and 67th Native Infantry: *2nd Brigade*, Lt. Col. Dickinson; HM's 80th (later 2nd Btn. South Staffordshires); 10th Native Infantry, 4th Sikh Regt. *3rd Brigade*, Lt.-Col. Huish; 101st (Bengal Europeans), 37th Native Infantry, Ludhiana Regt., 1 Light Field Battery
Madras Division, Brigadier-General S. W. Steel. *1st Brigade*, Col. Elliot; HM's 51st (King's Own Yorkshire Light Infantry); 9th and 35th Native Infantry. *2nd Brigade*, Brigadier-General McNeill; 102nd (Madras Europeans); 5th and 19th Native Infantry. *3rd Brigade*: HM's 84th; 30th and 46th Native Infantry; 1 troop Horse Artillery, 3 companies Foot Artillery, Sappers and Miners
16. *India Secret Proceedings*, no. 80, 27 May 1853
17. *Private Letters*, p. 259

CHAPTER 10
1. Gratton Geary, *Burma After The Conquest*, p. 154
2. John Cady, *A History of Modern Burma*, p. 118
3. *Letters From India*, vol. 45, 1885, p. 213, India Office Records
4. E. C. V. Foucar, *They Reigned in Mandalay*, p. 133
5. Cmd. 4614, p. 257
6. The three brigades under the command of Maj.-Gen. Prendergast were composed of the following infantry battalions:

Notes

   1st Infantry Brigade
      2nd Bn The Kings (Liverpool) Regt
      21st Madras Infantry
      25th Madras Infantry
   2nd Infantry Brigade
      2nd Bn. The Hampshire Regt
      12th Madras Infantry
      23rd Madras Infantry
   3rd Infantry Brigade
      1st Bn. Royal Welsh Fusiliers
      2nd (Queen's Own) Bengal Infantry
      11th Bengal Infantry
7. Foucar, op. cit., p. 157

Bibliography

Primary Sources

INDIA OFFICE LIBRARY
Bengal Secret and Political Consultations
Bengal Secret and Political Proceedings
India Secret Proceedings
India Political Proceedings
Letters from India: Political and Secret Series

PARLIAMENTARY PAPERS
First Anglo-Burmese War: *Papers Relating to the Burmese War*, February 1825
Second Anglo-Burmese War: *Papers Relating to Hostilities with Burma*, Cmd. 1490 (1852); *Further Papers relating to Hostilities with Burma*, Cmd. 1608 (1853)
Third Anglo-Burmese War: *Correspondence Relating to Burma since Accession of King Theebaw*, October 1878, Cmd. 4614 (1886)

The Burma Wars

Secondary Sources

BOOKS

Anon, *The Madras European Regiment in Burma*
Baird, J. G. A. (ed), *Private Letters of the Marquess of Dalhousie* (Blackwood, 1910)
Cady, John F., *A History of Modern Burma*, Cornell University Press, 1960
Crawfurd, J., *Journal of an Embassy to the Court of Ava*, London, 1834
Desai, W. S., *History of the British Residency in Burma*, University of Rangoon, 1939
Doveton, F. B., *Reminiscences of the Burmese War, 1824-26*, Allen & Co., London, 1852
Fortesque, J. W., *History of the British Army*, vols. XI, XII, Macmillan, London, 1923
Foucar, E. C. V., *They Reigned in Mandalay*, Denis Dobson, London, 1946
Geary, Grattan, *Burma after the Conquest*, London, 1886
Gouger, Henry, *Personal Narrative*, London, 1860
Hall, D. G. E., *Burma*, Hutchinson, London, 1960
Laurie, W. F. B., *The Second Burmese War*, Smith, Elder, London, 1853
Marshal, J., *Naval Operations in Ava*, Longmans, London, 1830
Maung, Htin Aung, *The Stricken Peacock*, Nijhoff, The Hague, 1965
Phayre, Arthur, *A History of Burma*, London, 1832
San Germano, Father Vincentius, *A Description of the Burmese Empire*, Constable, London, 1883
Smith, Vincent A., *The Oxford History of India*, Clarendon Press, Oxford, 1920
Snodgrass, J. J., *Narrative of the 1st Burmese War*, Murray, London, 1827
Symes, Michael, *An Embassy to the Court of Ava*, London, 1800
Wayland, F., *A Memoir of Judson*

Bibliography

Wilson, H. H., *Documents Illustrative of the Burmese War*, Calcutta, 1850
——*Narrative of the Burmese War, 1824-26*, W. H. Allen, 1852
Woodman, Dorothy, *The Making of Burma*, Cresset Press, London, 1962

JOURNALS

Journal of the Burmese Research Society, all volumes, especially:
Desai, W. S., 'Events at the Court and Capital of Ava During the 1st Anglo-Burmese War', *Journal of the Burmese Research Society*, vol. XXVII
Tanner, O. M., 'Danubyu', *Journal of the Burmese Research Society*, XXIX, 2, 1939

Index

Abercromby, Sir Ralph, 34
Alexander, Captain, 99, 100
Alompra, King of Burma, 8, 121
Amherst, Lord, 15, 20, 27, 34, 54, 97, 127
Aeng Pass, 97, 147-8
Anarchy, 131
Annexation, 132, 146, 153-4
Arachne, 73, 75, 83
Arakan,
  key frontier position, 4, 7-12
  War 1
    Burmese attack from, 41-5
    British attack, 94-7
    cession in peace talks, 112, 121, 129
  War 2, 147
Arakanese refugees, 4, 8-10
Armistice, 111-12
Artillery,
  British, War 1
    Assam, 39, 40-2
    Danubyu, 99, 102-7
    Irrawaddy, 117
    Kemmendine, 51, 54, 57-64
    Martaban, 74-6
    Shwedagon Pagoda, 85-7
    Thantabain, 73
    transport problem, 94-5
  British, War 2, 140
  British, War 3, 156
    see also howitzers and rockets
  Burmese, 17, 18, 32-3, 79, 83-4, 86-91, 130
    see also jingals
  elephant transport, 3, 18, 39, 41-2, 79
  Native regiments,
    Bengal, 73, 75
    Madras, 49

Assam, 13, 39, 41, 94
Astrology, 67, 71-2, 108
Austen, Admiral, 140
Ava,
  Court of, 1-2, 4, 7, 69
  War 1, plans to reach, 78, 91-4, 109, 125
  War 3, British troops in, 158

Bagyidaw,
  character of, 21, 48-9, 130
  as King by divine right, 1-3, 19-20, 25-6, 31
  deposed by rebellion, 130
  War with British, 2, 12-14, 46-8, 107-8
  see also Bundula
Peace,
  false offer of, 109
  talks, 111, 120-5, 126
  poverty after, 129
Bamboo, resistance to round-shot, 62
Bassein, 145
Bengal forces, 28, 140, 164, 166
  see also artillery, infantry and Sepoys
Bennett, Ensign, 45
Bentinck, Lord William, 130-1
Birch, Captain Richard, 49-50
Bodawpaya, King of Burma, 4, 5, 7, 8-12, 21
Body Guards, 113, 125
Bogle, Colonel, 138
Bombay-Burma Corporation Fine, 152, 154
Brandon, Captain, 43
Brisbane, Commodore Sir James, 114, 116, 117
Bucke, Major, 97-8

Buddhism, 21, 23-4, 48, 161
Bundula Mahâ,
  character, 77
  disciplinary measures, 77-8, 105
  death, 107
  memorial, 120
  war plans, 2-4
    Arakan, 41-6
    Assam, 13
    Danubyu, 71-9, 98, 100, 104-7
    Kemmendine, 80, 82-5, 87
    Kokeen, 88-9
    Manipur, 12
    Shwedagon Pagoda, 80, 81, 85-6
Burmese,
  Expeditionary Force, 27, 28, 164
  culture, 6, 12, 21-6, 150, 160
  warfare, 17-20, 52, 74
    see also entrenchment, fire rafts, night attacks, stockading and war boats
Burney, Major Henry, 130-1

Cachar, 4, 12, 13
Campbell, Ensign, 41
Campbell, General Sir Archibald,
  optimism of, 28-9, 32-4, 67
  peace,
    hopes, 67, 91, 94
    talks, 109, 111, 120-6
  risks taken by, 57, 59-60, 90, 99
  sickness, 63
  at war,
    Ava, plan to reach, 91, 94-5
    Danubyu, 98-103
    Irrawaddy Valley, 94, 97, 99
    Kemmendine, 50, 55, 57-63
    Kokeen, 90
    Martaban, 74
    Pagoda Point, 65
    Prome, 113-15
    Rangoon, 31-7, 47
    Shwedagon Pagoda, 49-55, 79, 82, 86
    Simbike, 115
    Thantabain, 73
Canning, Captain, 8, 9, 27
Cannon, Captain, 103
Carey, Colonel, 156

Cavalry,
  British, 39, 99, 156
  Burmese, 44-5, 79
Chads, Captain, 73, 86
Cheape, Brigadier-General, 149, 166
Chin Pyan, 8-10
Chittagong, 4, 7, 9, 13, 40, 45
  Provincials, 40-1, 43, 44
Cholera, 40, 63, 66-7, 118, 140, 145, 149
Churchill Lord Randolph, 154, 156
Class system, 22
Climate, 16-17, 26
  see also rainy season
Commander-in-Chief, British, in India
  see Paget, General Sir Edward
Commercial dispute leading to war, 3, 152
Conference, British/Burmese, 59
Conscription, 16, 70-1
Cotton, Brigadier-General Willoughby, 90-1, 99-103, 109, 116-18, 120, 125
Cotton, Major, 145
Cox's Bazaar, 95
Crisp, Mr, 133
Customs,
  Burmese, 6, 12, 21-3
    see also social structure
  diplomatic, 134-6

Dacoits, 130, 160
Dalhousie, Lord, 132-9, 145-8, 149-150
Dalla, 67, 81, 136
Danubyu,
  Bundula's forces at, 71-9, 91
  British attack, 98-9, 100-3, 106-7
Declaration of war,
  British, 15, 137, 156
  Burmese, 4, 139-40
Desertions, Burmese, 88, 117
Diana, 28, 91, 99, 105, 120
Discipline, Burmese army, 19-20, 77-78, 105, 117
Disease, 63-4, 66-7, 74, 76
  see also cholera dysentery and malaria
Divine right of Kings, 2-3, 23

Index

Dog spearing as pastime, 69
Doveton, Ensign reports,
  Dress, 53
  Kemmendine, 58-62, 83-4
  Rangoon, 32-4, 66
  Tenasserim, 68-9
Dress, 52-3, 157
Drunkenness, 36, 98
Dufferin, Lord, 153, 154
Dysentery, 63, 66-7, 74, 98

East India Company, 10, 27, 133
Elephants, 3, 18, 40, 41, 79, 147
Elrington, Colonel, 117
Engy Teekien, Crown Prince, 6
Entrenchment warfare, 17-18, 43, 51, 81-2, 86
Evans, Major, 73

Feroze, 146
Fire, 36, 89, 103
Fire rafts, 64, 80, 82, 84
Fox, 137, 141
Fraser, Lieutenant, 65-6
French, British fears of, 5-8, 13, 152-154
Freycinet, M. de, 154
Friendliness, Campbell's hope for, 28-9, 32, 34
Frith, Major, 57

Goats, 6
Godwin, Lieutenant-Colonel (later Lieutenant-General)
  War 1, 54, 65, 74-6
  War 2, 140-6
Gold as symbol, 1-2, 22-3, 36
Gouger, Henry, 3, 47
Governor-Generals,
  see Amherst, Bentinck, Dalhousie, Hastings, Minto, and Wellesley
Grant, Commodore, 27, 28, 36, 55
Griffiths, Major, 143
Grigg, Lieutenant, 45
Gweg-Yaung Kamyo, 156-7

Hastings, Lord, 11-13
Hermes, 136
Hinduism, 23

Hlaing River, 99
Hodgson, Colonel, 57
Howitzers, 28, 51, 54, 143-4, 156-7

India/Burma frontiers 2, 5, 7-14, 16, 37, 39, 94
Infantry,
  forces at,
  Arakan, 94, 165
  Assam, 39
  Chittagong, 39-44
  Danubyu, 104
  Kemmendine, 57-63, 80
  Martaban, 74, 75
  Pagoda Point, 65, 66
  Prome, 113
  Ramu, 41-2
  Rangoon, 34, 49, 140, 142
  Tenasserim, 68
  Thantabain, 73
  Wattygoon, 113
regiments,
  British,
    1st, 79
    2nd, 165
    13th, 34, 61, 82, 91, 117, 125
    38th, 34, 49, 54, 61, 73, 104, 117, 125
    41st, 34, 57, 61, 65, 74-5, 125
    44th, 165
    47th, 79, 117
    51st, 142
    54th, 165
    87th, 116-17
    89th, 49, 60, 68, 100, 125
    102nd, 58, 63, 113
  Native,
    13th, 40, 61
    17th, 65
    20th, 40-4
  Bengal Native,
    7th, 14th, 39th, 44th, 45, 52, 165
    18th, 40th, 144
    23rd, 39-44
  Madras Native, 60, 74, 75, 113, 164
    3rd, 74
    5th, 9th, 35th, 140
    7th, 68

Infantry—(cont.)
   17th, 65
   18th, 82
   26th, 80, 104
   38th, 117
   43rd, 125
Invulnerables, 72-3, 79
Irrawaddy Valley, 94, 99, 103, 116-117, 142
Italian fortification experts, 156-7

Jingals, 18, 79, 144
Joazoang, 51, 52
Judson, Adoniram, 25, 48, 70, 131
Judson, Mrs Anne, 46, 47

Kamaroot, 65, 66
Karen people, 149
Kee Wungyi, 47, 111-12, 115, 116, 121, 124
Keele, Lieutenant Charles, 74, 75
Kellett, Lieutenant, 83, 84, 91
Kemmendine,
   British attack, 49-50, 57-9, 60-4, 79, 80
   Burmese attack, 80, 82-5
Kengee Awengee, Bomein, 70
Kerr, Lieutenant Thomas, 50
Kinwun Mingyi, 151, 155, 158, 159
Kokeen, 88-91
Kolein Menghi, 121-3
Kykloo, 73

Lambert, Commodore, 132-7
Larne, 27, 28, 33, 63, 67, 73
Latter, Captain, 144
Laurie, Lieutenant, 141, 143-5
Liffey, 27, 28, 32, 33, 34, 36, 49
Loganunda Pagoda, 125
Looting, 36, 159

Macbean, Colonel (later Brigadier-General), 28, 54, 65-6, 96
McCreagh, Colonel, 28
McDowall, Colonel, 113
McMorine, Brigadier, 39, 40
Madras forces, 28, 60, 61, 74, 75, 113, 140, 164
   see also artillery and infantry
Magic attributed to British, 69-70

Magwe surrender, 157
Malaria, 63, 66-7, 74, 98
Mandalay, 152, 154, 157, 158
Manipur, 4, 12, 13, 95
Marryat, Captain Frederick, 28, 33, 55, 63-7
Marshall, Lieutenant John, 102
Martaban, 74-6, 140-1
Maysmore, Assistant surgeon, 45
Memiaboo, Prince of Tharrawaddy *see* Tharrawaddy
Merchants, complaints, leading to war, 132-3
Mercury, 57
Mergui, 68, 74
Mindon Min, 147, 148, 151
Minhla, 119, 120, 156, 157
Minto, Lord, 9-10
Mon people, 149
Monarchy, Burmese, 21, 26, 159-160
Monsoons *see* rainy season
Morrison, Brigadier-General, 94-8, 118, 165
Mughs, 10-11, 40, 43, 44, 79
Murder accusations, 132
Myat-Htoon, 149
Myingyau, 158

Naaf River, 41, 42-5, 96
Napadi, 114-16
Naval forces,
   War 1,
     Arakan, 94
     Assam, 39
     Dalla, 67
     Danubyu, 99-100, 102, 105
     Kemmendine, 57-9, 80, 83, 84
     Kokeen, 91
     Martaban, 74, 75
     Napadi, 114-16
     Pagoda Point, 63, 67
     Rangoon, 27-8, 49, 54-5
     Siriam, 67
     Thantabain, 73
   War 2, 136-7, 140-5, 146
   War 3, 156
Na-Wing Phuring, 125
Nemiao Mahâ, 112, 113-15
Neoun-ben-zeik, 111

Index

Night attacks (Burmese), 40, 51, 64-65, 82, 104
Noton, Captain, 41-5
Nyaungu, 157

Oakes, Major, 142
Optimism, 28-9, 32-3, 34-5

Paddy fields, 51-2
Pagan, 125-6, 158
Pagan Min,
  becomes King of Burma, 131
  conspiracy to dethrone, 147, 148
  War 3, 134-5, 138-9
Paget, General Sir Edward, C-in-C in India, 15-16, 26-7, 39, 45, 54, 97, 127
Pagoda Point, 65
Pakan-Woon, 108-9
Panhlaing, 99, 100
Peace
  War 1,
    Campbell's hopes for, 67, 91, 94
    talks,
      false rumours of, 88-9
      Minhla, 120-6
      Prome, 109-12
      Yandabo, final settlement, 126
  War 2,
    Dalhousie's hopes for, 138-9
    Mindon Min's hopes for, 139, 148
    Meeaday talks, 148

Pegu, 145
Pegu Province, 146-9
Pegu River, 113
Pemberton, Lieutenant, 95
Petition to avoid War 2, 137-8
Phayre, Captain, 147, 148, 149-50
Phlegethon, 137
Piper, Major, 64
Piracy of King's yacht, 135-7
Prendergast, Major-General Sir Harry, 154-60
Prince of Wales, 99
Pringle, Captain, 45
Prome,
  War 1, 101, 109-10, 112
  War 2, 146, 148
Protocol, disregard leading to War, 135
Provincials (Chittagong), 40-1, 43, 44

Queen,
  of Bagyidaw, 21, 107-8, 130
  of Mindon Min, 151, 154, 157-9

Rainy Season, 39-40, 49-55, 74, 77, 95-8, 109
Rajah of Manipur, 12, 95
Rajahs aid to Bundula's army, 41
Ramree Island, 96, 98
Ramu, 41-2
Rebellion, 130-1, 160
Rangoon,
  Symes' Mission, 5
  War 1,
    British entry into River, 27, 31
    British attack, 32, 37, 49, 55
    see also Shwedagon Pagoda
    Reinforcements, 93-4
  War 2,
    commercial situation leading to, 132-4
    Governor snub leading to, 133-7
    blockade, 134, 135
    see also Shwedagon Pagoda
  War 3,
    commercial affair leading to, 154
    forces assemble, 156
Regiments *see* artillery and infantry
Reid, Major, 142
Reignold, Colonel, 146
Reparations, 133-6
Richards, Lieutenant-Colonel, 40, 61, 94, 118
Robertson, Lieutenant, 61
Rocket,
  supplies, 57, 79, 94
  warfare, 102, 106-7, 117
Rose, Captain, 102-3
Ryves, Captain, 59, 80

Sale, Major, 82, 86, 99
Salisbury, Lord, 153-4
San Germano, Father, 19-20

Sandoway, 96, 98
Sappers, 140, 143
Satellite, 99
Scaling ladders, need for, 57, 59-60
Scorched earth policy, 101, 118-19, 127
Scott, Lieutenant, 41
Seindoop, 118
Sepoys, 40, 44-5, 51, 63-5, 74, 78, 113
Serpent, 141
Shan troops encouraged by women, 114-15
Shapland, Colonel, 40, 45
Shapuri, Island of, 13
Shuldham, Brigadier, 94, 95
Shwedagon Pagoda,
  War 1,
    occupation of, 35-6, 49
    Bundula's approach, 80, 81, 85
    Campbell's counter-attack, 86
  War 2, 142, 143-5
Siam, 4
Siriam, 54, 67
Sladen, Colonel, 159
Slaney, 27
Smith, Colonel, 57
Smith, Dr, 144
Snodgrass, Major (Military secretary to C-in-C) reports,
  Burmese army customs, 71-3, 81, 114
  Irrawaddy desertions, 101
  Kemmendine, 59
  Kokeen, 91
  Peace talks, 112, 121
  Rangoon, 33, 35, 81
Social structure, Burmese, 21-6
  collapse of, 150, 160
Sophie, 27, 64, 80, 84
Steel, General, 147
Stockades,
  Dalla, 67
  Danubyu, 101-2, 104
  Irrawaddy, 116-17
  Joazoang, 52
  Kemmendine, 49-51, 55, 57-60
  Kokeen, 90
  Naaf River, 41
  Rangoon River, 32, 54, 65, 66, 143-145

Thantabain, 73-4
Stockading, 18, 53
Supayalat, Queen, 151, 154, 157-9
Supplies,
  for Ava march, 118
  capture of, 85-7, 91
  restricted by scorched earth policy, 101, 118-19, 127
  for Danubyu, 99, 100, 105-6
  at Rangoon,
    limited for entry, 27-8
    inadequate at, 35, 37
  reinforcements, 93-5
Sylhet frontier, 94
Symes, Colonel Michael, 4-8, 18-19, 25

Talaings, 145
Taingda, 151, 154
Talek Pass, 97
Tarleton, Commander, 145, 146
Tavoy, 68, 74
Teak log export affair, 152
Tenasserim district, 68-9, 74
  cession in peace talks, 112, 121, 129
Teignmouth, 80, 82, 83, 84
Terrain, 16, 26, 39, 95
Thantabain, 73-4
Tharrawaddy,
  Prince as army leader, 71, 73, 74, 78, 109, 118, 124
  King by deposing Bagyidaw, 130-131
  failure as, 131
Tharrawaw, 99, 100
Thetis, 57, 59
Thibaw, King of Burma, 151, 154, 157-9
Thooreah, 159
Tilsit, Treaty of, 7
Tonghoo, Prince of, 71
Toungoo, 147
Treaty,
  commercial, 129-30, 131-2
  peace *see* peace talks
  Tilsit, 7
Trueman, Captain, 42, 45

Umbrella as symbol, 22, 81, 140

Index

Viceroy of Pegu, 11, 15

Wahab, Major, 65
Walker, Major, 86
War,
  boats, Burmese, 18-20, 84, 100, 103
  declaration, *see* declaration
Warfare, British and Burmese compared, 52
  see also Burmese warfare
Wattygoon, 113
Wellesley, Governor-General, 4-8
Wilkinson, Lieutenant James, 49-50
Wolsely, Ensign Garnet (later Lord), 149

Yandabo peace settlement, 126
Yates, Major, 80, 82, 83, 84

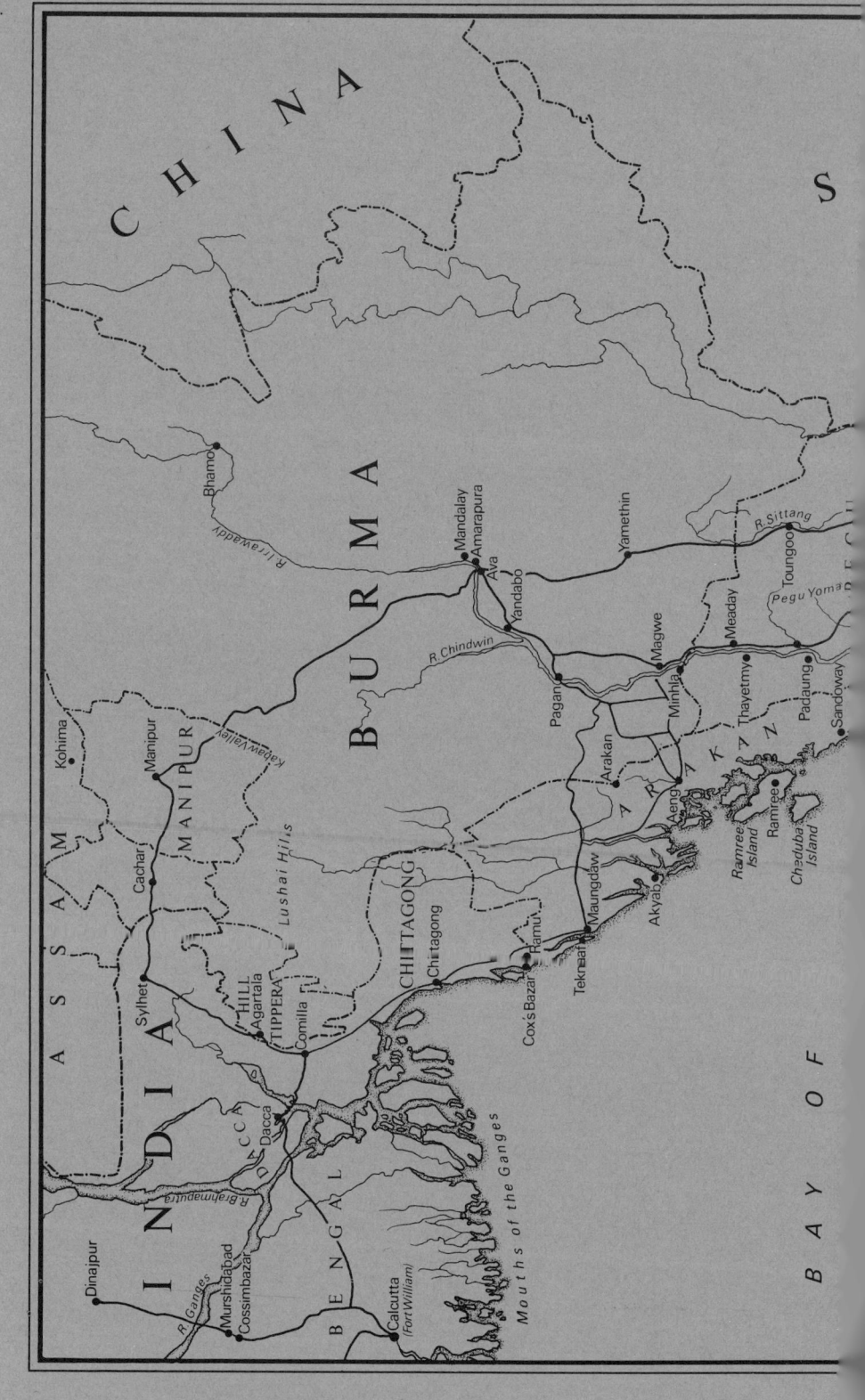